Writing the Critical Essay

SMOKING

An OPPOSING VIEWPOINTS® Guide

Writing the Critical Essay

SMOKING

An OPPOSING  VIEWPOINTS® Guide

Other books in the Writing the Critical Essay series are:

Alcohol
Animal Rights
Cloning
The Death Penalty
Energy Alternatives
Terrorism

Writing the Critical Essay

SMOKING

An **OPPOSING**  **VIEWPOINTS**® Guide

Mary E. Williams, *Book Editor*

Bruce Glassman, *Vice President*
Bonnie Szumski, *Publisher, Series Editor*
Helen Cothran, *Managing Editor*

**OPPOSING
VIEWPOINTS**®
SERIES

GREENHAVEN PRESS
An imprint of Thomson Gale, a part of The Thomson Corporation

THOMSON
*
GALE

Detroit • New York • San Francisco • San Diego • New Haven, Conn. • Waterville, Maine • London • Munich

© 2006 Thomson Gale, a part of The Thomson Corporation.

Thomson and Star Logo are trademarks and Gale and Greenhaven Press are registered trademarks used herein under license.

For more information, contact
Greenhaven Press
27500 Drake Rd.
Farmington Hills, MI 48331-3535
Or you can visit our Internet site at http://www.gale.com

LIBRARY OF CONGRESS CATALOGING-IN-PUBLICATION DATA

Smoking / Mary E. Williams, book editor.
  p. cm. — (Writing the critical essay)
    ISBN 0-7377-3204-0 (lib. bdg. : alk. paper)
    1. Smoking—United States. 2. Tobacco industry—United States. 3. Essay—Authorship. 4. Rhetoric. I. Williams, Mary E., 1960– II. Series.
    HV5765.S66 2006
    362.29'6—dc22

                                         2005049313

Printed in the United States of America

CONTENTS

Section Three: Supporting Research Material

Examining the state of writing and how it is taught in the United States was the official purpose of the National Commission on Writing in America's Schools and Colleges. The commission, made up of teachers, school administrators, business leaders, and college and university presidents, released its first report in 2003. "Despite the best efforts of many educators," commissioners argued, "writing has not received the full attention it deserves." Among the findings of the commission was that most fourth-grade students spent less than three hours a week writing, that three-quarters of high school seniors never receive a writing assignment in their history or social studies classes, and that more than 50 percent of first-year students in college have problems writing error-free papers. The commission called for a "cultural sea change" that would increase the emphasis on writing for both elementary and secondary schools. These conclusions have made some educators realize that writing must be emphasized in the curriculum. As colleges are demanding an ever-higher level of writing proficiency from incoming students, schools must respond by making students more competent writers. In response to these concerns, the SAT, an influential standardized test used for college admissions, required an essay for the first time in 2005.

Books in the Writing the Critical Essay: An Opposing Viewpoints Guide series use the patented Opposing Viewpoints format to help students learn to organize ideas and arguments and to write essays using common critical writing techniques. Each book in the series focuses on a particular type of essay writing—including expository, persuasive, descriptive, and narrative—that students learn while being taught both the five-paragraph essay as well as longer pieces of writing that have an opinionated focus. These guides include everything necessary to help students research, outline, draft, edit, and ultimately write successful essays across the curriculum, including essays for the SAT.

Using Opposing Viewpoints

This series is inspired by and builds upon Greenhaven Press's acclaimed Opposing Viewpoints series. As in the parent series, each book in the Writing the Critical Essay series focuses on a timely and controversial social issue that provides lots of opportunities for creating thought-provoking essays. The first section of each volume begins with a brief introductory essay that provides context for the opposing viewpoints that follow. These articles are chosen for their accessibility and clearly stated views. The thesis of each article is made explicit in the article's title and is accentuated by its pairing with an opposing or alternative view. These essays are both models of persuasive writing techniques and valuable research material that students can mine to write their own informed essays. Guided reading and discussion questions help lead students to key ideas and writing techniques presented in the selections.

The second section of each book begins with a preface discussing the format of the essays and examining characteristics of the featured essay type. Model five-paragraph and longer essays then demonstrate that essay type. The essays are annotated so that key writing elements and techniques are pointed out to the student. Sequential, step-by-step exercises help students construct and refine thesis statements; organize material into outlines; analyze and try out writing techniques; write transitions, introductions, and conclusions; and incorporate quotations and other researched material. Ultimately, students construct their own compositions using the designated essay type.

The third section of each volume provides additional research material and writing prompts to help the student. Additional facts about the topic of the book serve as a convenient source of supporting material for essays. Other features help students go beyond the book for their research. Like other Greenhaven Press books, each book in the Writing the Critical Essay series includes bibliographic listings of relevant periodical articles, books, Web sites, and organizations to contact.

Writing the Critical Essay: An Opposing Viewpoints Guide will help students master essay techniques that can be used in any discipline.

Background to Controversy: How Smoking Became Popular in America

Tobacco smoking most likely originated in the Western Hemisphere. The tobacco plant (*Nicotiana tabacum* and *Nicotiana rustica*) grows naturally in North and South America and was cultivated by native peoples hundreds of years before the arrival of European explorers. Some groups, such as the Caribs of the Caribbean islands, snuffed a tobacco mixture through a tube called a *tobago,* which is probably the root of the word *tobacco.*

The natives' taste for tobacco eventually caught on with the European adventurers who came to the Americas in the late 1400s and thereafter. These explorers took tobacco back to their home countries of Spain, Portugal, France, England, and Holland. They also began cultivating the plant near sea routes—in places as distant as the Philippines and southern Africa—to secure a supply of tobacco on future voyages. Thus, through explorers and merchants, tobacco smoking spread rapidly around the world.

Tobacco Use in the United States

Fueled by European demand, tobacco became a lucrative commercial crop in the American colonies during the 1600s and 1700s. Enormous tobacco plantations, worked by thousands of slaves, sprang up in the Chesapeake region and near the southeastern coastline. Tobacco products were commonly used as currency and helped finance the Revolutionary War.

While pipes and snuff were popular during the colonial period, chewing tobacco and cigars became the trend during the early days of the United States. It was not until the 1860s, during the Civil War, that cigarettes ("tiny cigars") came into vogue. Cheaper and more convenient than cigars, soldiers adopted cigarette smoking as a way to escape from the hardships of battle. When they returned home from the war, soldiers introduced cigarette smoking to their friends, and a growing number of civilians took up the habit.

The wars of the twentieth century also helped to spread cigarettes widely across American society. During World Wars I and II smoking was encouraged among U.S. soldiers, as cigarettes were said to provide comfort and boost morale. In the 1940s President Franklin D. Roosevelt declared tobacco an essential crop and allowed tobacco farmers to be taken off of draft lists to ensure continued tobacco production. Cigarettes were included in the field rations of ground troops, and a majority of soldiers, sailors, and pilots smoked.

More Americans at home became smokers as well—invited and encouraged by catchy cigarette ads featured on billboards, on the radio, in movies, and in magazines and newspapers. During the first half of the twentieth century, these ads promoted cigarette smoking as a healthy and attractive activity. Even medical magazines,

Many smoking advertisements of the early twentieth century, such as this one featuring 1920s athlete Bob Beattie, promoted smoking as a healthy activity.

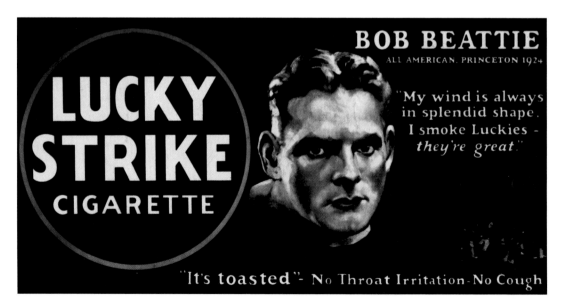

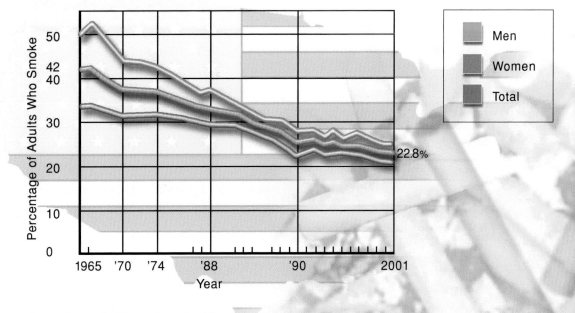

Smoking Rates Among U.S. Adults

Percentage of Adults Who Smoke

Men
Women
Total

22.8%

Year

1965 '70 '74 '88 '90 2001

Source: Centers for Disease Control and Prevention, U.S. Census Bureau, 2004.
Data not available for all years.

including the *Journal of the American Medical Association,* accepted tobacco advertising, which stated, "We advertise KOOL cigarettes simply as a pleasant combination of fine tobaccos made even more pleasant by the cooling sensation of menthol. They won't cure anything. They won't harm anybody. They will prove enjoyable." Between 1940 and 1950 cigarette consumption doubled in the United States. By 1950 three out of four men smoked, half that number of women smoked, and nearly eight hundred thousand teenagers were taking up smoking each year.

Criticisms of Cigarettes

By the middle of the twentieth century, researchers had gathered some startling statistics on cancer and smoking. Between 1930 and 1950, for example, deaths from lung cancer quintupled. Even though the *Journal of the American Medical Association* had accepted cigarette advertising, it

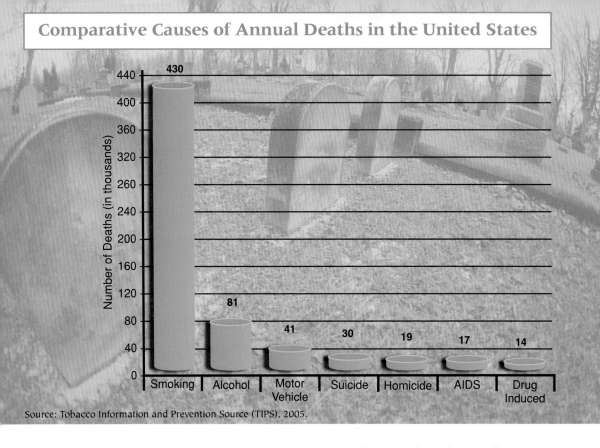

Comparative Causes of Annual Deaths in the United States

Number of Deaths (in thousands)

- Smoking: 430
- Alcohol: 81
- Motor Vehicle: 41
- Suicide: 30
- Homicide: 19
- AIDS: 17
- Drug Induced: 14

Source: Tobacco Information and Prevention Source (TIPS), 2005.

published an article in 1950 showing that almost all patients with lung cancer had been longtime cigarette smokers. Scientists undertook multiple studies on the effects of cigarette smoking, culminating in the release of a report by the U.S. surgeon general in 1964. On the basis of more than seven thousand studies, this report concluded that smoking causes lung and laryngeal cancer, chronic bronchitis, heart disease, and emphysema. Armed with this information, the federal government began to take steps to restrict tobacco advertising. By 1966 cigarette packages were required to carry warnings about the hazards of smoking. In 1971 radio and television ads for cigarettes were banned.

Many Americans heeded the government's health warnings, and by the 1990s the percentage of adult smokers in the population had decreased to 25 percent. After more research suggested that nonsmokers' health was threatened by inhaling the secondhand fumes of cigarette smokers, smoking was banned on all domestic airplane flights.

In addition, several cities and states have prohibited smoking in restaurants, bars, and indoor workplaces.

Although the percentage of American smokers decreased over the course of the twentieth century, deaths from tobacco-related illnesses are at epidemic proportions. According to the Centers for Disease Control and Prevention, 430,000 Americans die annually from smoking-related diseases—more than the yearly deaths resulting from drug abuse, AIDS, traffic accidents, fires, murder, and suicide combined. Concerns about the effects of smoking have motivated health-care advocates, politicians, and ordinary citizens to organize a variety of antismoking campaigns.

The antismoking movement made huge strides in the 1990s when the courts found the tobacco industry responsible for damaging the health of its customers.

Lawsuits Against Tobacco Companies

The 1990s proved expensive for tobacco companies. Early in the decade various groups sued the tobacco industry for knowingly contributing to smoking-related illnesses and deaths. In 1997 the state of Florida settled its suit with the industry for $11 billion; Minnesota for $6 billion; and Mississippi for $3.4 billion. Sixty thousand flight attendants also settled their case for $300 million. The Master Settlement Agreement of 1998 required the four largest tobacco companies to pay $206 billion over twenty-five years to compensate forty-six states for smoking-related health costs. The tobacco industry also agreed to fund a five-year, $1.5 billion antismoking campaign and to abide by certain marketing restrictions, including an end to the use of cartoon characters and other youth-oriented sales strategies, large-scale outdoor ads, and the sale of logo-emblazoned merchandise.

Antismoking groups have mixed feelings about the tobacco settlement. While they applaud the marketing restrictions, they note that the tobacco industry still spends about $8 billion a year on advertising. They also maintain that tobacco companies continue to promote smoking to youths through the sponsorship of sporting events and concerts, by ads in magazines that are geared to people over eighteen but that are also read by teenagers and children, and by product placements in movies that young people watch. However, not all anti-smoking advocates believe that cigarette ads are the most significant factor in encouraging people to smoke. Many believe that peer and parental influences affect a young person's decision to smoke more than any advertisement does.

The Current Debate

As the following selections show, much of the continuing debate over tobacco focuses on concerns about the health effects of smoking and what might influence people, especially youths, to decide to smoke.

Section One:
Opposing
Viewpoints
on Smoking

Smoking Should Be Condemned

Dean P. Johnson

In the following essay Dean P. Johnson uses descriptive detail to denounce the habit of smoking. He recalls growing up with parents who smoked and who later died as a result of tobacco-related illnesses. Early on he enjoyed the rituals associated with his parents' smoking and began smoking himself as a child. Later Johnson realized that smoking and secondhand smoke led to the untimely deaths of his parents and still threaten his health and the health of his siblings. Johnson teaches English at Camden Academy Charter High School and at Rowan University in Glassboro, New Jersey.

Consider the following questions:

1. How would Johnson imitate his father on Sunday afternoons?
2. How old were the author's parents when they died?
3. According to doctors cited by Johnson, why is secondhand smoke especially toxic?

I half smiled when I heard the report about a Virginia woman who was sentenced to 10 days in jail for smoking in the presence of her children.

That's because my parents smoked.

Every night after dinner, my mother and father would lounge on the couch and put a match to a cigarette.

I remember watching them and feeling a little envious. It was like they were having another dessert. They seemed to enjoy it so thoroughly, and they looked so good doing it too.

They are young in this memory, their hair still dark, their faces still smooth, their bodies slender and strong. I remember sitting on the floor, just watching them, anxious for the day when I would be allowed to smoke.

The Splendor of Smoking

We had ashtrays all through the house. The good ones were made of thick green or golden-bronze glass. There was a plastic one in the bathroom that sat on the back of the toilet or sometimes on the rim of the sink next to where we kept our toothbrushes. We even had a large ashtray with a fancy J on it, like a royal stamp. Whenever my father jinked his ash, his Army ring banged against the glass ashtray, making a tinkling sound and creating the illusion that the cigarette itself could chime.

Children who are exposed to secondhand smoke can develop serious health problems.

I mostly enjoyed Sunday afternoons when my father would sit on the floor in front of the television, lean against the footstool and watch whatever sport happened to be in season. He would fix himself a tray of peanuts in the shell; a bottle of beer; a fresh, stiff pack of cigarettes and an ashtray.

I would often sit next to him with a bottle of soda and pretzel sticks that I would pretend were cigarettes.

There was a sunbeam that would slant through the living room window in the afternoon, slicing through the smoke that was always there. I loved watching the minuscule particles in a hazy spotlight, dancing in wild splendor.

Sneaking Cigarettes

Once, when no one was looking, I took two cigarettes from my dad's pack. My best friend Curt and I ran down into the woods and lighted them up. The menthol taste was

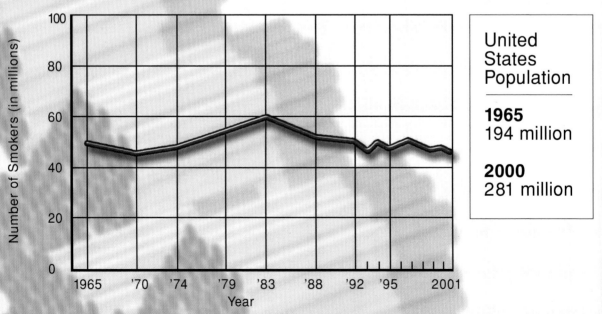

Number of Smokers in the U.S.

Although smoking rates have declined in the United States since 1965, the actual number of smokers has not changed dramatically because the overall population has grown.

United States Population

1965
194 million

2000
281 million

Number of Smokers (in millions)

Year

Source: Centers for Disease Control and Prevention, U.S. Census Bureau, 2004. Data not available for all years.

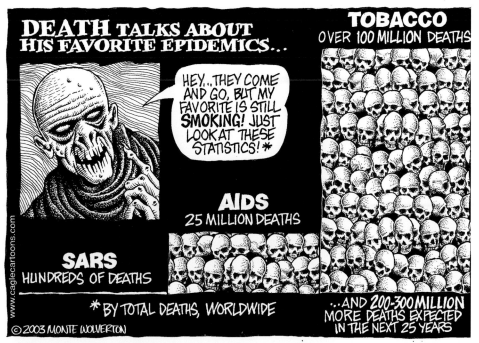

Wolverton. © 2003 by Cagle Cartoons, Inc. Reproduced by permission.

so offensive to us that we could not get beyond a few puffs. "Let's try my dad's," Curt suggested, and he pulled out two regular cigarettes.

"Mmmmm, now that's a cigarette," I said.

Curt and I continued sneaking cigarettes from his dad as often as possible.

We even, upon occasion, bought our own packs. Because both of our fathers used to send us to the store to pick up a pack of cigarettes for them, like our moms would send us for a loaf of bread, it was easy and there were never any questions asked.

When I was in sixth grade, my mother stopped smoking. She told my brothers and me that it was a nasty habit. "But Dad smokes," we said. It's bad for him too, she said.

I never remember seeing my mother with a cigarette in her hand again.

My father continued smoking—one to two packs a day. I smoked off and on from about the fifth grade through college.

Organs Affected by Smoking

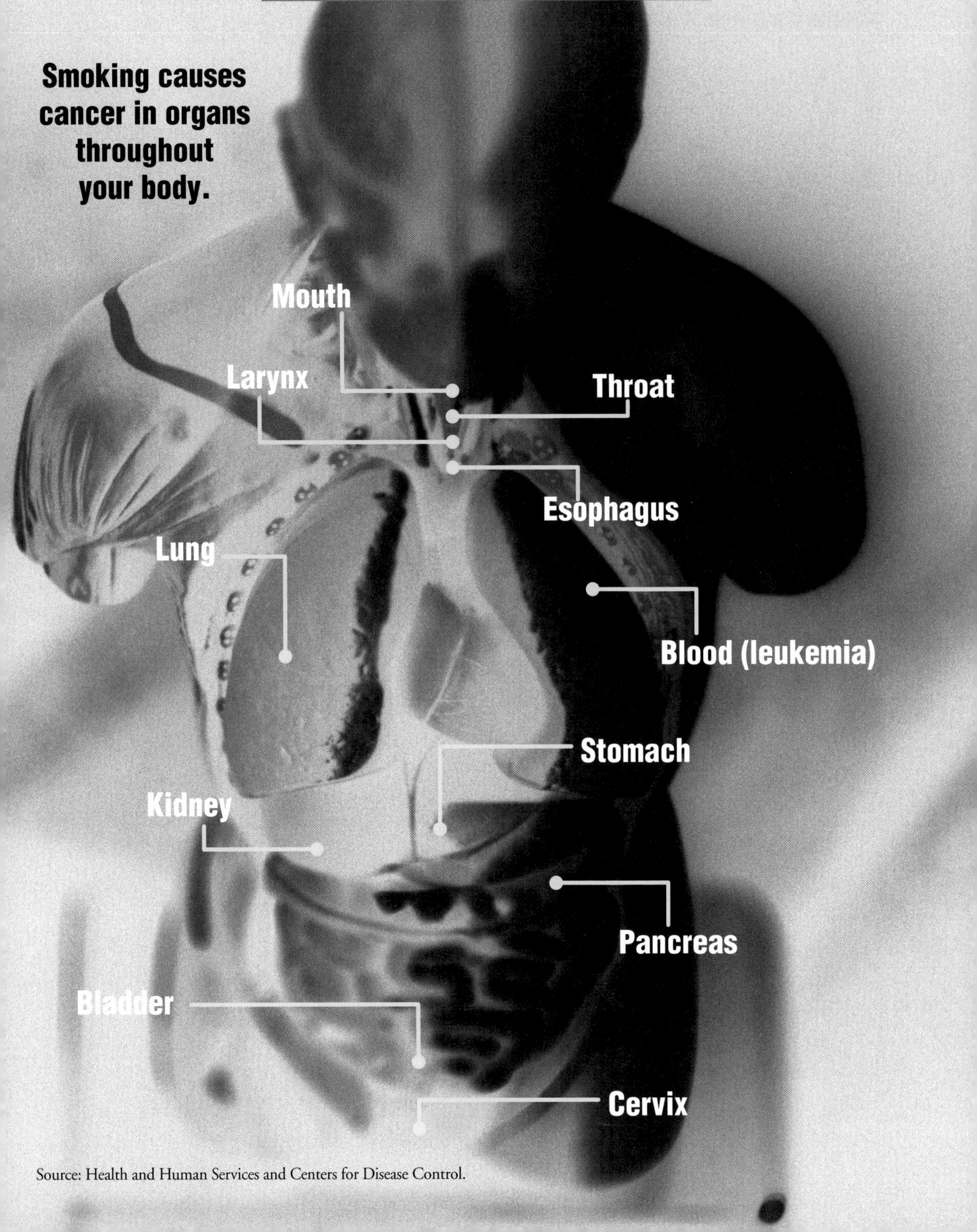

Smoking causes cancer in organs throughout your body.

Mouth

Larynx

Throat

Esophagus

Lung

Blood (leukemia)

Stomach

Kidney

Pancreas

Bladder

Cervix

Source: Health and Human Services and Centers for Disease Control.

Untimely Deaths

When my father died of bladder cancer at the age of 56, it was clear that his smoking was a direct cause of his demise. The nicotine concentrates in the bladder, the doctors said, bathing the organ in carcinogens. When my mother died of lung cancer at 56, only 17 months after my father, it was clear that my father's smoking was a direct cause of her early demise as well. Secondhand smoke, the doctors explained, is often more toxic because it is unfiltered.

The most beautiful smoke that balleted through the air—plié, pirouette and sissonne—ribboning with elegance in certain slants of light on Sunday afternoons was that unfiltered smoke that danced into my mother, my brothers and me from the warm, glowing tip of my father's cigarettes.

Ten days in jail for smoking around one's own children may seem like a severe punishment, but it just may be what it will take to beat an early death sentence.

Analyze the essay:

1. In your opinion, what are the most effective descriptive details in this essay? Explain.
2. Do you think Johnson truly believes that parents should be sentenced to jail for smoking in the presence of their children? Why or why not?

The Tobacco Industry Should Not Be Condemned

Mario Vargas Llosa

Since tobacco has never been illegal, the tobacco industry should not be punished for cigarette-related health problems, argues Mario Vargas Llosa in the following essay. Drawing on his experience as a former smoker, Vargas Llosa admits that some people choose to engage in destructive habits even when they are fully aware that their health is endangered. Because they are informed about the harms of tobacco, individuals in free democratic societies are responsible for making their own decision to smoke, he concludes. Vargas Llosa is an internationally acclaimed novelist, politician, and playwright from Peru.

Consider the following questions:

1. Why did Vargas Llosa continue smoking even after his first "disgusting" experience with cigarettes?
2. What led the author to admit that "human beings are even more stupid than we seem?"
3. Although he no longer smokes, why does Vargas Llosa now feel a sense of solidarity with smokers?

Although, since I stopped smoking 30 years ago, I have detested cigarettes and their manufacturers, I have not been as pleased as other ex-smokers to see damage awards in lawsuits against tobacco companies reach the hundreds of billions of dollars, for reasons I would like to try to explain.

Mario Vargas Llosa, "A Languid Sort of Suicide," *New York Times*, September 1, 2000. This article, which appeared in a longer form in the Spanish newspaper *El Pais*, was translated by James Brander. Copyright © 2000 by The New York Times Company. Reproduced by permission.

From Disgust to Felicity

In Cochabamba, Bolivia, when I was 7 or 8, my cousins Nancy and Gladys and I invested our allowances in a packet of Viceroys and smoked them all. Gladys and I survived, but the weakling Nancy began vomiting, and her grandparents had to call the doctor. This first smoking experience greatly disgusted me, but my passion for being grown up was stronger than the disgust, and I went on smoking.

My adolescence at university is inseparable from the oval-shaped Nacional Presidente brand with its piquant black tobacco, which I smoked incessantly while reading, watching movies, arguing, falling in love, conspiring or attempting to write. Drawing in the smoke and blowing it out, in rings or as a cloud that dissolved into dancing figures, was a great felicity: a companion, a support, a distraction, a stimulus.

Three Packs a Day

When I arrived in Paris in 1958, the discovery of Gitanes catapulted my tobacco habit, and soon I was smoking

Sharpnack. © 1999 by Joe Sharpnack. Reproduced by permission.

Many smokers are aware of the health risks involved with cigarettes, but they believe it is their right to make the choice to smoke.

three packs a day. After a strong coffee and a croissant, the first drag of thick smoke had the effect of the true awakening, the start-up of the organism. A lighted cigarette in the hand was an indispensable prerequisite for any action or decision: opening a letter, answering a telephone call, requesting a loan at the bank. I took the last drag of the day when already half-way asleep.

A doctor warned me that cigarettes were harming me; I was tormented by bronchial problems, and the Parisian winters kept me sneezing and coughing incessantly. I paid no attention to him, convinced that without tobacco my life would be terribly impoverished and that I might even lose my urge to write. But on moving to London in 1966, I tried a cowardly compromise, trading the beloved Gitanes for the blond Players No. 6, which had a filter and less tobacco and which I never really liked.

Quitting

It was my neighbor, a medical professor, in the town of Pullman, Wash., who finally made me decide to stop smoking. I was in that remote place of snowstorms and red apples as a visiting professor, and he asked me one day to go with him to his office. I warned him that I was genetically allergic to conversions, but went. For three or four hours he gave me a practical lecture against cigarettes. I returned convinced that human beings are even more stupid than we seem, because smoking constitutes an unmitigated cataclysm for any organism, as anyone may see who takes the trouble to consult the encyclopedic scientific information on the subject. Perhaps what most impressed me was the absolute disproportion which, in the case of the cigarette, exists between the pleasure obtained and the risk run, unlike other practices, also dangerous to health, but infinitely more succulent than the foolery of breathing smoke in and out. Still, I went on smoking for at least a year more, in an agitation of fear and remorse every time I lit up.

I quit the day in 1970 that I left London to go and live in Barcelona. It was less difficult than I had feared. The first weeks I did nothing else but not smoke—it was the only activity in my head—but it was a great help, from the first moment, to begin to sleep like a normal person and to wake up in the morning feeling fresh. It was most amusing to discover there were different smells in life—that the sense of smell existed—and above all, flavors, that is, that a steak did not taste the same as a plate of chick peas.

An Antismoking Apostle

Quitting smoking did not at all affect my intellectual work; on the contrary, I was able to work longer hours without the chest pains that used to wrench me away from the writing desk. The negative consequences were appetite, which burgeoned, obliging me to exercise, diet and even fast; and a certain allergy to the odor of tobacco, which, in countries where people still smoke a lot and smoke everywhere, as in Spain or Latin America, may complicate life for the ex-smoker.

As often occurs with converts of the tiresome sort, for a while I became an anti-tobacco apostle. In Barcelona, one of my first conquests was [Colombian novelist] Gabriel García Márquez who, one night, livid with horror at my missionary stories about the havoc wreaked by nicotine, threw a packet of cigarettes on the floor and swore he would never smoke again. He kept his promise.

My zeal waned over the years, especially when, in much of the world, campaigns against cigarettes proliferated and the matter began, in certain countries like Britain and the United States, to assume a complexion of paranoia and witch-hunting. Nowadays it is impossible, in these countries, not to feel a certain civic solidarity with the smokers.

The Freedom to Choose

It is, of course, quite fair that the tobacco companies should be penalized if they have concealed information or have used prohibited substances to increase addiction. But is it not hypocrisy to consider them enemies of humanity while the product they offer has not been the object of a specific prohibition by law? Nor should there be such a prohibition.

The obligation of the state, in a democratic society, is to make citizens aware that tobacco is harmful, so that they can decide with adequate knowledge whether to smoke. This, indeed, is what is happening in most Western countries. If a person in the United States, France, Spain or Italy smokes, it is not out of ignorance of what this means for health, but because he does not wish to know, or does not care.

In 1998 actor/ comedian Drew Carey protests California's smoking ban by lighting up in a Hollywood restaurant.

[The choice to] commit suicide by degrees is a choice that ought to figure on the list of basic human rights. This is the only possible approach if we wish to preserve the freedom of the individual, which must include the freedom to opt not only for what is beneficial to him, but also for what harms or injures.

And so, though at first sight, the decision of juries to impose astronomical penalties on the tobacco companies may seem a progressive measure, it is not so. What sort of freedom would it be that allowed us only to choose what is good for us?

Analyze the essay:

1. What are the most compelling descriptive passages in this essay, in your opinion? How does Vargas Llosa enable the reader to experience his relationship to smoking?
2. Why do you think the author goes into such detail about his life as a smoker and his experience of quitting smoking? How does his story lend support to his argument against punishing the tobacco industry?

Cigarette Ads Encourage Youths to Smoke

John DiConsiglio

In the following piece John DiConsiglio maintains that tobacco companies use advertising to encourage young people to try cigarettes. While these companies can no longer place ads in magazines created specifically for teenagers and children, they still advertise in fashion, sports, and music magazines that are made for adults but are also read by youths. Tobacco companies also target minors through glamorous images of smoking in movies and television shows, by selling candy-flavored cigarettes, and by offering free music and games of interest to youths, the author notes. Research proves that these ad campaigns are effective. DiConsiglio is a freelance writer based in Washington, D.C.

Consider the following questions:

1. What kind of damage can one cigarette do, according to researchers cited by the author?
2. Why do tobacco companies target teenagers in their ads, according to DiConsiglio?
3. According to Amanda Feldman, quoted by the author, what is the best way for youths to combat tobacco advertisers?

Myth: Most young people smoke.

Fact: A recent survey of teens done by the U.S. Surgeon General's office found out that only 13 percent of those polled had smoked in the previous 30 days.

John DiConsiglio, "Smoke Screen: Why Do Tobacco Ads Look Glamorous and Sexy—When Everyone Knows Smoking Is Gross?" *Scholastic Choices*, vol. 20, February/March 2005. Copyright © 2005 by Scholastic, Inc. Reproduced by permission.

Myth: Smoking is sexy and attracts others.

Fact: Kissing a smoker is a bad experience. Smoking causes bad breath, yellow teeth, and wheezing.

Myth: Smoking will not affect my health.

Fact: Just smoking one cigarette can damage your DNA, say researchers at the University of Pittsburgh. Smoking also causes diseases like lung cancer and emphysema.

Cigarette advertisements often feature beautiful, healthy-looking people in order to attract customers to their product.

Myth: The health warning on cigarette packs is small and simple; smoking can't be that big of a deal.

Fact: There are four different warnings. The Federal Trade Commission requires tobacco companies to rotate them on both their ads and their packs.

Myth: You can smoke while you're young and stop before damaging your health.

Fact: A Chapel Hill Center of the Pacific Institute for Research and Evaluation study shows that kids who smoked only one cigarette by the fifth grade were nearly twice as likely to be current smokers by age 17.

Unrealistic Ads

Flipping through a *Vogue* magazine one day, Thania Balcorta quickly scanned articles on shoes and hairstyles and barely glanced at the photos of the models. But one page made her pay attention. It was a cigarette advertisement. In it, a group of young people laughed around a pool table. At the center was a skinny model in leather pants. Her face was obscured, but something about the picture made Thania think the girl was beautiful. And the way she held the tip of the pool cue also brought an image to Thania's mind. It looked like a cigarette.

The ad was not a realistic portrayal of smokers. No one had yellow teeth or was coughing. And no one looked like they smelled of stale smoke. The point of the ad wasn't just to sell cigarettes. It was also selling an idea. "The ad was saying that I could be thin and pretty and have fun too—if I smoked," Thania, 16, says.

At the time, many of Thania's friends were smokers. The ad hit a nerve with Thania. "It made me want to smoke," she [says]. Thania, who lives in Davis, California, resisted the urge to light up. Instead, she joined the American Legacy Foundation, a nonprofit group involved with antismoking ads.

Courting Teens

Now, Thania talks to her peers about the subtle methods tobacco advertisers use to turn teens into smokers. "Teens

The cartoon character Joe Camel was used in countless cigarette advertisements before such images were banned in 1998 on the grounds that they target children.

are being manipulated," Thania says. "Tobacco companies will do anything to get a cigarette in our mouths."

Tobacco companies deny that they target teens as customers. And you won't find cigarette ads in magazines that are produced for teenagers and younger kids. But there are magazines for adults that cover topics such as fashion, sports, music, TV, and the movies that kids are interested in. And many of these publications do have cigarette ads. *Vogue* is just one example. There are many others, including *Sports Illustrated*, *Rolling Stone*, *Vibe*, and *Entertainment Weekly*. Kids read these magazines.

Sell, Sell, Sell

Smoking is big business. And young people are lighting up. Each day, nearly 4,400 kids between the ages of 12 and 17 in the United States start smoking, according to the Centers for Disease Control and Prevention. The Campaign for Tobacco-Free Kids reports that almost 90 percent of adult smokers started the habit before they were 18.

There are many reasons why kids start to smoke, including peer pressure and parental influence. Antismoking activists say that the multibillion-dollar advertising campaigns promoting smoking also lure kids to try smoking.

"Tobacco companies are juggernauts," says Phil Graham, director of marketing for the American Legacy Foundation. "They are the most well-funded mass marketers. They know exactly what buttons to push to make teens start smoking. And they aren't afraid to push them."

There's evidence to support that claim. A 1981 document from Philip Morris, the maker of Marlboro cigarettes said, "Today's teenager is tomorrow's potential regular customer." For years, tobacco maker R.J. Reynolds ran ads starring a cartoon character named Joe Camel. Studies showed that he was as recognizable to five-year-olds as Mickey Mouse.

But in 1998, 46 states sued the largest cigarette makers and forced them to stop advertising to teens. By law,

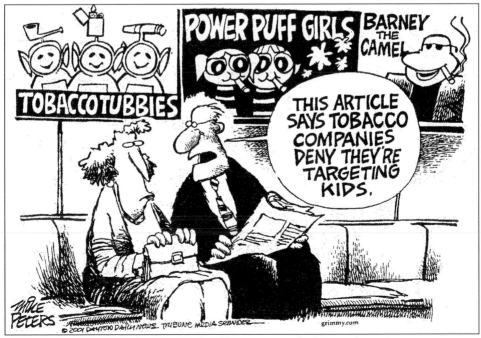

Peters. © 2001 by *Daytona Daily News*. Reproduced by permission of Tribune Media Services.

the companies had to tear down billboards, pull ads in teen magazines, and stop using cartoons to promote cigarettes.

Smart Tactics

But, according to antismoking groups, the law hasn't stopped tobacco firms from targeting teens. They've just become more clever at it. Besides advertising in magazines aimed at adults that teens read, tobacco firms also place their ads in places frequented by young people.

"Go into a convenience store and you'll find the cigarettes right next to the candies, where only a little kid would see them," Graham says.

Tobacco companies also market flavored cigarettes, with names like Midnight Berry, Mocha Taboo, and Twista Lime. "Their products are clearly aimed at kids," says Danny McGoldrick, research director for the Campaign for Tobacco-Free Kids. And, this past summer [of 2004], the makers of Kool cigarettes were forced to scale back their "Kool MIXX" hip hop tour. Three states sued Kool for targeting kids with DJ competitions, free CDs, and games, and cigarette packs decorated with hip hop designs.

"They want you to think of smoking as fun and cool," says Andre Vidler, 18, of Rockland County, New York, who helps teens in her school watch for hidden smoking messages.

"They want you to feel like a loser if you're not in the big smoking party."

How It Works

Few teens admit that advertising influences them. Indeed, it's hard to trick media-savvy kids who are skeptical of big business sales pitches. But advertising is complicated. It's not just a matter of see-the-ad-smoke-the-cigarette. Advertisers work hard to create an image around a product.

"The ads are designed to create an aura of smokers," says Peter DeBenedittis, an advertising expert and pres-

Actor Brad Pitt smokes in a scene from the 2000 film, Snatch. *Movies frequently feature characters who smoke.*

ident of Media Literacy for Prevention. Girls who see ads with beautiful models associate that look with smoking. Boys who see pictures of tough men are sent the not-so subtle message that real men smoke.

And it's not just magazine ads. An American Legacy survey found that more than half of all teens see a glamorized portrayal of smoking on TV or in the movies at least once a week. "Cigarettes look pretty neat when Brad Pitt lights one up," Graham says.

Do these schemes—misleading ads, cool giveaways, flavored cigarettes, movie-star smoking and product placement in stores—really work? An American Legacy survey found that teens are three times more likely to be affected by tobacco ads than adults—and twice as likely to remember the ads a week later. A Dartmouth University study showed that young people were 16 times more likely to use tobacco if they saw their favorite actor smoking.

Lighting Up

And while teen smoking rates actually dropped by 5 percent between 2000 and 2002, about 4.5 million kids under 18 still smoke. Every time Amanda Feldman, 17, walked into the bathroom of her high school in Lynnwood, New Jersey, she'd smell smoke. When she strolled along the bike path after school, she'd pass packs of teen smokers.

Amanda volunteers with antismoking groups to help open kids' eyes. "The ads make it seem like, if you're smoking, you're doing your own thing," she says. "But you're not. You are doing what tobacco companies want you to do."

The best way to combat the smoking advertisers is to inform yourself, says Amanda. Ask why you see images of smoking in magazines and movies. Why are tobacco companies making candy-flavored cigarettes? And why don't those young, vigorous people in the smoking ads look like the pale, sickly smokers you know in real life? "It's all a lie," Amanda says. "But we're smart enough to see through it."

Analyze the essay:

1. According to DiConsiglio, what specific elements make cigarette ads attractive to young people? Do you find the techniques that tobacco advertisers use persuasive? Why or why not?
2. Do you think antismoking organizations such as the American Legacy Foundation can reduce the effectiveness of tobacco advertising? Why or why not?

Antitobacco Ads Discourage Youth Smoking

Peter Vilbig

Recent antitobacco campaigns are persuading youths to avoid smoking, reports Peter Vilbig in the following selection. As part of a 1998 lawsuit settlement, the four largest tobacco companies are required to fund advertising that discourages youth smoking. According to Vilbig, these antismoking ads, which employ sarcasm and dark humor, are effective because young people have helped create them. Although teenagers are still bombarded with cigarette ads, antitobacco forces remain confident that they will reduce youth smoking, the author concludes. Vilbig is a freelance journalist.

Consider the following questions:

1. What percentage of high school seniors smoke daily, according to the author?
2. How much money are states receiving from tobacco companies as a result of the 1998 legal settlement, according to Vilbig?
3. According to Vilbig, what do the ads created by the Truth and Target Market campaigns focus on?

Rodriguez Barnett could easily have been a teen smoker. The 17-year-old high school senior from St. Paul, Minn., comes from a tobacco-using family: His father, brother, and sister are all smokers, and his mother quit only after recent heart problems. When he was younger, big tobacco companies were using kid-friendly mascots such as Joe Camel, a pack of cigarettes was relatively cheap, and youth smoking was on the rise.

But Barnett hates Big Tobacco. Of course, he knows about the obvious health risks—at this point, who doesn't? What sent him over the edge, motivating him to do spoken-word performances for Target Market, a Minnesota anti-tobacco youth campaign, was the deceit.

"My take is I'm being targeted by the tobacco companies," Barnett says, "and I don't like people manipulating my mind."

David Versus Goliath

Barnett has become a warrior in a modern-day battle of David and Goliath. On the Goliath side are U.S. tobacco companies, which spend $8 billion a year to make smoking appear sexy, sophisticated, and mature. On the David side are anti-tobacco groups, many of them involving teens, that can only spend a fraction of that amount, but have effectively used a series of edgy ads—at a time of higher prices for cigarettes and greater restrictions on where smoking is allowed—to help drive a steep drop in teen smoking.

After climbing in the early 1990s, teen smoking rates have fallen by nearly half for 8th-graders, a third for 10th-graders, and more than 20 percent for 12th-graders.

But in a sign that Goliath is far from dead, teen smoking rates remain high. Thirty percent of high school seniors are occasional smokers, and 19 percent smoke daily. (About 25 percent of the adult population smokes regularly.)

Tobacco companies insist they don't target teens in their marketing campaigns. But critics say the tobacco industry depends on hooking the ranks of the young, because once they start smoking, the odds are high that they will continue lighting up for years, possibly for life.

"Tobacco companies know teens are where the money is," says Jeff Arnett, an independent scholar at the University of Maryland who has testified in numerous

Minnesota governor Jesse Ventura participates in the state's Tobacco Prevention Day in 1999. Such antismoking events are a popular way to discourage young people from smoking.

anti-tobacco lawsuits. "They know that if they get them at 14, they'll have them at 24 and 44." The Surgeon General reports that among current smokers, 80 percent started before they were 18.

Recently, the percentage of teens who say smoking is a health hazard has leveled off, in what could be "an early warning sign" that the slowdown in teen smoking is over, according to a University of Michigan study.

Paying for Their Own Decline

The anti-tobacco campaign has its roots in the 1998 settlement of a huge lawsuit brought by 46 states. The four largest tobacco companies agreed to pay the states $206 billion over 25 years. The agreement settled charges alleging that the companies had repeatedly lied about the safety of their products, creating billions of dollars in health care expenses nationwide.

The settlement had one immediate effect: The companies passed along the cost to customers, bringing a steep rise in the price of cigarettes. With the average pack today costing more than $3, the sticker shock may account for a portion of the decline in teen smoking. A National Cancer Institute study released [in 2002] found that even a 10 percent increase in cigarette price could reduce youth smoking by 5 percent, a much higher rate than for adults.

An antismoking advertisement by the edgy campaign known as "Truth." The Truth campaign was started by the tobacco industry as part of the 1998 Master Settlement Agreement.

The tobacco companies also gave rise to a multimedia anti-tobacco campaign calling itself "Truth." Thanks to the settlement, the campaign comes literally at the expense of the companies. Tobacco companies, already prohibited by federal law from advertising on TV, agreed to stop all print advertising aimed at teens and to fund the American Legacy Foundation, which created the Truth campaign. The foundation now has an annual advertising budget of more than $100 million.

The result is a series of ads that are a far cry from your parents' anti-smoking ads. The new ads don't nag about the health dangers of smoking, a tactic teens say doesn't work. "The 'horrific death' thing has been played out," says Diane Tran, 18, a senior from Lakeville, Minn., and a member of Target Market, itself funded by the tobacco settlement. "It's 'Don't do that,' and nobody listens."

> ## The "Truth" Brand
>
> The "truth" brand builds a positive, tobacco-free identity through hard-hitting advertisements that feature youths confronting the tobacco industry. This rebellious rejection of tobacco and tobacco advertising channels youths' need to assert their independence and individuality.
>
> Matthew C. Farrelly et al., *American Journal of Public Health*, June 2002.

A Message That Works

But teens are listening to the Truth ads, in part because they helped create them. The American Legacy Foundation has met with 100 teens repeatedly to help hone its campaign. Programs like Minnesota's Target Market and others in Florida, New Jersey, and Maine have also enlisted young people. The goal is to channel feelings of anger like Rodriquez Barnett's about dishonesty and manipulation.

The ads employ wicked sarcasm. They've used body bags, rat costumes, hidden cameras, and urinals to fashion some of the barbs. In one Truth radio ad, a teenager who claims to be a dog walker calls the offices of Lorillard Tobacco. Employees ask him his business, and he responds by offering to provide the cigarette maker with "quality dog urine." The reason: It contains urea, which, he says, is a chemical that is also put into cigarettes.

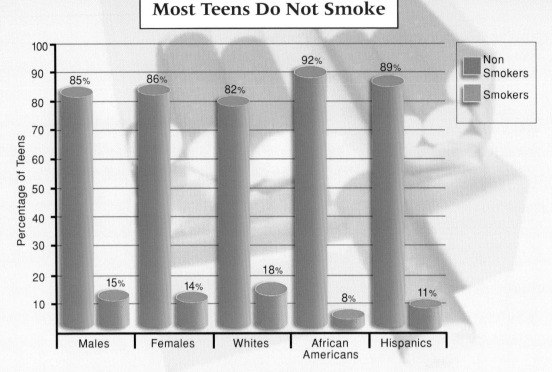

Most Teens Do Not Smoke

	Non Smokers	Smokers
Males	85%	15%
Females	86%	14%
Whites	82%	18%
African Americans	92%	8%
Hispanics	89%	11%

Percentage of Teens

Source: Centers for Disease Control and Prevention, www.cdc.gov, 2005.

Lorillard says urea is a natural ingredient in tobacco, not an additive. It sued the American Legacy Foundation, saying that the ad violated the settlement agreement's restrictions against direct attacks on the tobacco companies.

The tobacco companies have been grumbling since the foundation first broadcast a TV commercial portraying piles of body bags in front of Philip Morris's headquarters in 2000. They say they aren't targeting teens anymore, so why are teens targeting them? "We are making a responsible effort to target only adult audiences," says Steve Watson, a spokesman for Lorillard, reflecting the views of many in the industry.

Tobacco Promotion Continues

But anti-tobacco forces say teens are still bombarded with tobacco ads in high-teen-readership magazines like *Rolling Stone*, *People*, *Sports Illustrated*, and others. A recent study by the California Attorney General found that 12- to 17-year-olds see 50 cigarette ads per year in magazines alone. That doesn't include the cigarette promotions teens see in convenience stores, gas stations, and similar locations.

An especially powerful promotional tool has not been banned: smoking in movies. Critics say it's basically a commercial when a star lights up in a hit film. "As good as the anti-tobacco campaigns are, they cannot compete with one actor on the screen," says Susan Moses, director of the Harvard Tobacco Project.

Recently, tobacco opponents have met with movie executives in an effort to limit the on-screen smoking. Some advocates even want to shield teens by requiring an R-rating for movies in which actors smoke. Film studios so far have shown some willingness to consider voluntarily limiting cigarette smoking in films, but the R-rating looks like a long shot.

Still, the anti-tobacco forces are prepared to continue the big fight, believing they have what it takes to topple Goliath. "We've packaged Truth as a brand," says Lyndon Haviland, the chief operating officer of the American Legacy Foundation. "If you arm teens with the power, the facts, teens get it."

Analyze the essay:

1. Vilbig begins his article with an anecdote about a high school student. How does he make a transition from the introductory anecdote to the topic of his article?

2. Do you agree with Vilbig that the use of sarcasm in antismoking ads is more persuasive to youths than are warnings about the dangers of tobacco? Why or why not?

How I Got Hooked on Cigarettes

Dale Pray

In the following selection former smoker Dale Pray uses detail and narrative to describe how he became a regular smoker. He recalls childhood memories, such as being exposed to secondhand smoke, playing with candy cigarettes, and his mother using cigarette smoke to soothe his painful earaches. He also recounts how peer pressure led him to start smoking at the age of twelve. Pray offers this story on his personal Web site as a warning to others.

Consider the following questions:

1. When was Pray's first exposure to cigarette smoke?
2. How old was the author when he first tried cigarettes?
3. What percentage of smokers begins smoking before the age of twenty-one, according to Pray?

I was first exposed to cigarettes when I was in the womb. Mom was a smoker at the age of 16. She quit school and went to work in the shoe shop like many of her peers did at that time. You didn't need an education to work, jobs were everywhere. Cigarettes were cheap and a large percentage of the population smoked. It seemed that the worst health hazard from smoking at a young age back in that era was that perhaps it would "stunt your growth." Mom never grew more than 5 feet tall. (Probably just a coincidence.) Mom and Dad got married in [February 1954], shortly after I was "on the way." Folks back then were not aware of the dangers and risks associated with smoking while pregnant. So many of us smokers got our first dose of nicotine thru the umbilical cord.

A Cigarette Odyssey Begins

From my birth in [December] 1954 my odyssey with cigarettes began with exposure to secondhand smoke. Everywhere you went there was someone smoking. No one gave it a thought that perhaps the smoke-filled rooms and automobiles might harm the ones that didn't smoke. Smoking just seemed to me as a normal thing for grown-ups to do. I fully expected to become a smoker myself someday. Thanks to some candy manufacturers, I was able to simulate smoking by buying some candy cigarettes. I

In the 1950s the harmful effects of smoking were not yet widely known.

was very careful to hold it between my fingers like a real one and put the filter end in my mouth. The end you would light, if it was a real one, was dyed red to simulate the lit end. Candy cigarettes even came in the popular brands and similar styles that the real ones came in. This helped in establishing a loyalty to a particular brand at a young age I suppose. Now that I reflect back, I seem to recall a toy cigarette that would emit simulated smoke when a kid blew through it. I guess it made me feel good to emulate something that adults did.

I recall getting my first feeling of comfort from cigarette smoke when I was a toddler of perhaps 4 or 5 years of age. I suffered from horrendously painful earaches. I would wake up in the middle of the night with my inner ear throbbing with pain. I remember the sound of drumming, snapping and crackling inside my ears as the drainage from the ear infection would flow and the tissues were swelling. Inevitably I would cry out to Mom. Mom would take me in her arms and bring me to her rocking chair in the living room. She would light up a cigarette, inhale, then very gently blow the warm smoke into my hurting little ear. This always seemed to help relieve the pain, or at least make it bearable. After the cigarette treatment Mom would put a few warm drops of baby oil in my ear, insert a wad of cotton and rock me until I fell asleep. An act of love and compassion from mother to child that meant a lot to me back then, but would probably not be considered a good thing to do in case of earache now.

The Start of a Habit

I got my first actual puff on a real cigarette at around age 10. I recall a real boring afternoon visiting some relatives with my folks. The relatives didn't have any children at home. They had all grown up and moved on. So there I was bored out of my gourd, when I decided I would take a nap in the car while my folks finished their visit. That's when I noticed an ashtray with some partially smoked

A 20-story cigarette ad dominates the skyline in New York City in 1974.

butts and a cigarette lighter, right there in front of me. Curiosity got the better of me. I chose one of the longest stubs I could find, straightened out the kinks where it had been crushed out, and put it to my lips. I pushed in the cigarette lighter handle, like I had seen mom do many times, and waited for the familiar click that signaled when the lighter was hot enough to light a cig. I took the cherry red tip of the lighter and placed it on the end of the cigarette butt and sucked. I got a mouthful of the foul hot smoke, blew it out, and wondered what the attraction of cigarettes was supposed to be. They tasted awful. I don't think I tried them again for several more years.

When I was around 12, I started delivering *TV Guides* to homes around town to earn some money. I would always be on the look out for bottles to cash in for the deposit. I also got an allowance from my folks for doing chores around the house. It was great having some coin in my pocket to buy Slim Jims, popsicles and Beatle trading cards. One summer afternoon I was out delivering my *TV Guides*. One of my customers had a boy a year older than I was, Jim was his name. His parents were not home, but Jim invited me in to hang out with him and his buddies. They were playing cribbage for cigarettes. I didn't know how to play cribbage but Jim offered to teach me and even gave me a few cigarettes to get started. Well I must of had one massive case of beginners luck, because an hour or so later I was the owner of a pile of cigarettes.

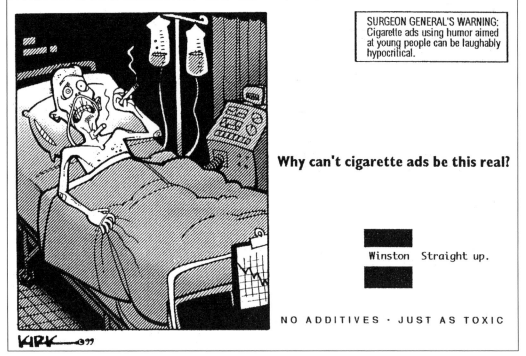

Kirk. © 1999 by Kirk Anderson. Reproduced by permission.

I was also the owner of a brand new habit that would haunt me for many years. I was well on my way to becoming addicted to cigarettes.

I didn't inhale at first, just sucked in the smoke and blew it out. One day another of my smoking buddies asked me If I inhaled. I said no, I really didn't realize that was part of smoking. He said to take a puff on the cig and then just breathe it back into the lungs. I tried it and choked and coughed and got dizzy like everyone does when they first inhale. But I was determined to keep it up until I could smoke with the best of them. Why didn't I take that strong hint that my body was trying to give me, that CIGARETTES ARE BAD FOR YOU. Let's face it, the choke, cough, and gag reflex is a part of our bodies for a good reason. It is a body's natural defense mechanism shouting NASTY STUFF, FOUL AIR, UNNATURAL THING TO DO. . . . Yet peer pressure, wanting to be cool and do grown-up things gave me the incentive to keep on inhaling till I got it right and became thoroughly addicted to the proverbial cancer stick.

> ## Smoking Is a Form of Conformity
>
> **Teenagers who smoke are seeking to be like adults around them who smoke, and cigarette use is seen in many families and communities as a marker of adulthood.**
>
> Mike A. Males, *Smoked: Why Joe Camel Is Still Smiling*, 1999.

Sneaking Smokes

Winstons were my cigarette of choice. I remember a childhood version of the Winston song. "Winston tastes good like a cigarette should. No flavor, no taste, just a 30 cent waste." I used to buy Winstons for my Mom at the neighborhood stores. So naturally I bought the same brand so as not to arouse suspicion that I was the one I was buying cigarettes for. Even back in the mid-60s it was not considered good form for a 12 or 13 year old kid to be smoking. So we would find places around town that were out of sight and a kid could smoke away from the disapproving eyes of adults. Under the bridge in the center of town or up on the railroad trestle were good spots to smoke. At any given time there was always someone there you could smoke and joke with. Sharing a cigarette was kind of a social thing. You could always "bum a cig" if you needed one or you would give one to someone else who needed one. I very seldom had to bum, as I had my own *TV Guide* route, and eventually went on to sell newspapers as well. Some of the guys used to steal their cigs, either from a store or from their parents. Of course I never did, being the darling little angel that I was. . . .

By the time I was 16 I had permission to smoke, as was common back then. I am sure my folks knew I had been smoking for quite some time, but now I could smoke in the house. I didn't have to hide it, except at school. I remember sharing a cigarette with buddies in the bathroom. Someone would stand guard at the door scanning for teachers, while the other ones would huff down a quick cigarette. You had to be quick and make every hit count, especially if your next class was way on the other end of school. I was smoking over a pack of cigs a day.

The tobacco industry loses close to 5,000 customers every day in the US alone—including 3,500 who manage to quit and about 1,200 who die. The most promising "replacement smokers" are young people: 90% of smokers begin before they're 21, and 60% before they're 14!

Analyze the essay:

1. The author admits that a variety of factors influenced his decision to smoke. What are these factors? In your opinion, which of these factors had the greatest effect on him? Explain.
2. Pray describes several moments in his childhood that affected his attitude toward cigarettes. Examine one of these passages and note the words and phrases that depict sight, sound, touch, taste, and smell.

Why I Quit Smoking

Christina Fletcher

In this essay freelance writer Christina Fletcher discusses her introduction to cigarette smoking as a young girl and how she became a regular smoker while attending community college and working as a waitress. Even though she suffered from asthma attacks, cigarettes became her constant companion. She decided to quit when it became painfully obvious that smoking was damaging her health.

Consider the following questions:

1. Why did Fletcher decide to try cigarettes?
2. When did the author first notice that smoking was affecting her ability to breathe?
3. Why did Fletcher continue smoking even after her emergency room experience?

The first time I smoked a cigarette, I was 13 years old. I lived with my mother and brother on Laurel Avenue in Liverpool, New York, and was walking home with a friend. We saw this crisp blue-and-white pack of cigarettes just sitting on the side of the road and were curious. So we picked it up and opened it to find half a pack of cigarettes left. My friend and I joked around about trying to smoke. But by the time we got to my house, we still hadn't actually lit up, and we just ended up going our separate ways.

Since I was the one who still had the pack, I decided to experiment on my own. It wasn't really that I wanted to be a smoker—I had grown up with all the messages about how bad cigarettes are for you just like everyone

Christina Fletcher, "Smoking Almost Killed Me," *CosmoGirl!*, vol. 4, November 2002. Copyright © 2002 by Hearst Communications, Inc. Reproduced by permission.

Smoking is very
common at clubs,
bars, concert halls,
and other
establishments all
over the world.

else. But I did want to try smoking, just so I'd know what it was like. I liked doing daring things like skateboarding and going on biking adventures. Smoking my first cigarette kind of felt like that.

I remember going to the garage so no one would know. I looked around to make sure I was alone, and then lit a cigarette and sneaked my first puff—and started coughing like crazy. I thought it was the most disgusting-tasting thing ever, and I stamped the cigarette out. My hands had a putrid

smell from holding the burning cigarette, so I ran inside the house to wash them. A few days later, I told my mom that I'd tried smoking. (I tell her everything.) I said it was awful. And that I would never do it again. She was relieved.

A Life Change

I'd been a ballet dancer since I was five, and smoking really didn't fit into that world anyway. Dancers are health-conscious and try to take care of their bodies. My plan was to make a living as a ballerina.

A Symbolic Act

For a beginner, smoking a cigarette is a symbolic act conveying messages such as, in the words of the tobacco company Philip Morris, "I am no longer my mother's child," and "I am tough."

Martin J. Jarvis, *British Medical Journal*, January 31, 2004.

When I moved to Rochester the following year, I went to a special high school for dance. But soon I started feeling pain in my knees whenever I'd do a plié. The doctor said my kneecaps were deteriorating and I'd have to wear knee braces every time I danced. I didn't do that—I felt too self-conscious of the way they looked—so my knee problems got worse.

By the time I was 18, I gave up dancing (because of my knees) and decided instead to study criminal justice in college. I even thought I might join the FBI. I guess it was the daredevil in me again.

Smoking Away

After high school, my mom moved to Toronto, but I stayed in Rochester to attend Monroe Community College. I started hanging out with people from the local music scene. Aside from studying, I spent my time at smoke-filled clubs listening to live music. It was a very social and "cool" environment, and smoking was an integral part of it. Everyone I was interested in getting to know smoked, so I started smoking too. At first, I bummed cigarettes off people. But within a few weeks, I was smoking half a pack of cigarettes every day—and started buying my own cigarettes.

I liked smoking. I felt like I'd joined a club. Bumming a cigarette or a light was an icebreaker, a way for me to bond with people and to share with friends. Instead of confiding in a friend over a cup of coffee or a drink, I'd do it over a cigarette. Smoking also came to my rescue when I was nervous or felt out of place. When I took a drag, I'd get a little buzzed and feel less anxious. And the actual act of smoking occupied me—it made me feel like I was doing something instead of just standing around.

Cigarette smoking can often trigger a coughing spell, especially when a person first starts smoking.

The First Alarm

Even though I stopped dancing, I tried to keep in shape by running three times a week. But six months after I started smoking, I had trouble breathing when I ran. My chest would get really tight, and my heart would pound so hard

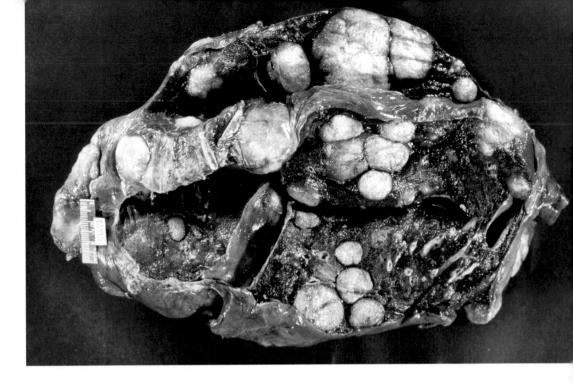

Pictured here is a human lung that is riddled with cancerous tumors caused by years of smoking.

that my body vibrated. I'd feel light-headed and start gasping for air, as if I were drowning.

I was diagnosed with asthma and given an inhaler to help my breathing. I never told my doctor that I smoked; I didn't think it mattered since I was only 19. The inhaler helped me run farther before I lost my breath. But still, by the time I finished my run, I'd be doubled over, unable to breathe.

Throughout college, I smoked more and more—until I was smoking a steady two packs a day at age 22. Part of the reason I smoked so much was that I worked as a waitress and a bartender (during college and after I graduated), so I was always around smokers. But it was also that cigarettes became my constant companion—they kept me company when I was studying, talking on the phone, and hanging out with my friends. Cigarettes were like makeup or a security blanket for me—they completed me, because they helped me feel more comfortable and relaxed no matter what I was doing. Taking a drag off a cigarette forced me to deeply inhale and exhale, which calmed me down and helped me feel more alert.

I also became much more permissive about my smoking. I never lived with my mother as a smoker, but even so, I refused to smoke in my house when I first started, because when I was younger, my best friend's parents smoked, and the tiles on their ceiling were yellow from it, which really grossed me out. But then I got a roommate who also smoked, and we would just sit at the dining-room table, drink coffee, smoke lots of cigarettes, and talk.

A Wake-up Call

Early that September, my friend and I went to see a Sunday night showing of *Buffalo 66*. I had a cold but was psyched to see the film. Just as the movie started, I felt a tickle in the back of my throat, which I tried to clear. At first, I tried to jiggle it with an "mm-hmm." When that didn't work, I gave a slight cough—which turned into a coughing fit I couldn't control. All of a sudden, I threw up. I put my hands to my mouth to try to catch it and wound up holding a bunch of mucus. I turned to my friend and said, "I just threw up. I have to get out of here." We got up and left.

During the 10-minute walk home, I just kept coughing uncontrollably—and I threw up a few more times. It was all happening so rapidly that I couldn't even breathe. That's when my friend insisted on taking me to the hospital.

When I got to the emergency room, I was hooked up to a machine, and I inhaled the steroid albuterol for an hour and a half to dilate my bronchial tubes and help me breathe again. At one point, a nurse came into the room and looked at me breathing with the machine. She asked if I was a smoker, and when I told her I was, she said, "I'm not trying to lecture you, but you'd better quit—unless you want to end up in here every single day doing this like some other patients I see."

All I did was laugh. It wasn't that I didn't believe her. I did. But I think she scared me so much that I became defensive and turned it all around, thinking who was she to just butt into my business. I just could not accept that I was causing myself such pain.

The Benefits of Quitting Smoking

The risk of stroke is reduced to that of a person who never smoked 5 to 15 years after quitting.

The risk of cancers of the mouth, throat, and esophagus is halved 5 years after quitting.

Cancer of the larynx risk is reduced after quitting.

Coronary heart disease risk is cut in half 1 year after quitting and is nearly the same as someone who never smoked 15 years after quitting.

Chronic obstructive pulmonary disease risk is reduced after quitting.

The risk of lung cancer drops by as much as half 10 years after quitting.

The risk of developing ulcers drops after quitting.

Bladder cancer risk is halved a few years after quitting.

Peripheral artery disease risk goes down after quitting.

Cervical cancer risk is reduced a few years after quitting.

The risk of delivering a low birth weight baby drops to normal if women quit before pregnancy or during the first trimester.

Source: Tobacco Information and Prevention Source (TIPS), 2005.

Cold Turkey

I continued to smoke two packs a day, and within a year, my asthma got so bad that I was having three attacks a day. (I used to get them about once a month.) I'd try to use my inhaler, but it didn't always work. What's scary about an asthma attack is that it comes on very suddenly, and you feel like you're suffocating. You get dizzier and dizzier because you literally cannot breathe. Imagine someone strangling you or putting a pillow over your face. The only difference is that when someone tries to suffocate you, you can struggle with them and at least try to push them off. With an asthma attack, you're helpless: You just can't get any air.

I was only 23 years old, and the continual pain was taking its toll. One morning, shortly after my attacks had gotten so bad, I woke up and immediately felt my lungs aching. They pulsated and felt bruised, like they'd been punched repeatedly. I felt every breath I took in my back, as if I had pneumonia. All of a sudden, I thought, Oh my God, I could get cancer and die. I could have lung cancer. It was the first time that thought had crossed my mind—and that very day, I tried to quit smoking.

It sounds clichéd, but quitting smoking was one of the hardest things I ever did, especially because I wanted to do it on my own, without any medication or support groups. I'd make it a few days, and then I'd be at the restaurant working, and everyone else would be smoking, and I'd just cave. I still wanted to be a part of that club. But starting again always made me disappointed in myself. I tried to quit four times before I was actually able to do it. My friends tried to encourage me to stick to it, and this one guy even bought me

> **Smokers Are in Denial**
>
> If smokers thought regularly about the toxins and carcinogens in cigarettes, we would all collapse in blubbering heaps every day, terrified of the cancer or heart disease that surely lurks around the corner.
>
> Dan Jenkins, "'How I Finally Gave Up Smoking,'" *Europe Intelligence Wire,* January 28, 2005.

a yo-yo to keep my hands busy. I lasted three weeks that time.

Success

On my fifth attempt at quitting, everything finally clicked— and I did it! Maybe I was just tired of always feeling so sick. Maybe it was because I finally went through my house and threw away all my ashtrays, as a sign of my determination. But what I think really made the difference was that I changed my patterns. I had developed a relationship with smoking, and I needed to break that. For a while, I stopped hanging out in places like bars, where I'd be tempted to smoke.

At first, every time I'd read the paper or talk on the phone, I'd want to smoke, and I'd have to tell myself no. But then, after two months, I just got used to not smoking. To be honest, my asthma got worse the first few months after I quit—but my doctor had warned me that would happen, because my lungs had to clear up.

It's been two years since I've smoked, and I can't remember when I had my last asthma attack. Smoking was such a part of me that I felt naked when I first quit. But now, when I'm around smoke, it bothers me—and I can't imagine ever having another cigarette.

Analyze the essay:

1. Fletcher was apparently diagnosed with asthma only after she began smoking. Do you think her story could convince smokers who do not have asthma to quit smoking? Why or why not?

2. What is the "turning point" in Fletcher's narrative description—the event that makes her decide to quit smoking? Does she create suspense as she describes the experiences that led to this event?

Section Two:
Model Essays
and Writing
Exercises

Writing the Descriptive Five-Paragraph Essay

Section I of this book gave you examples of published persuasive writing about smoking. All were opinionated essays offering various points of view on cigarette smoking and the tobacco industry. Most of these essays also used descriptions to convey their message. In this section, you will focus on developing your own descriptive-writing skills.

A descriptive essay paints a mental picture of the subject the writer is exploring. Typically, descriptive writing uses the five senses—sight, sound, touch, taste, and smell—to help the reader experience what the writer has experienced. A descriptive writer carefully selects vivid examples and specific details to reveal people, places, processes, events, and ideas. Details that include some aspect of the five senses are often called images.

While an essay can be purely descriptive, descriptive papers written for the classroom are often persuasive or expository essays that use description to make a point. Published writers may also rely on description as they explain something or voice an opinion, especially if they are writing about people, places, or past events. For example, in Viewpoint 1, Dean P. Johnson maintains that smoking should be condemned. To support his argument, he describes his memories of growing up in a household of smokers, how he began smoking, and, finally, his reservations about secondhand smoke. His concise descriptive passages, full of unique details and creative illustrations, engage the reader while voicing an opinion about smoking.

In the following section you will read some model descriptive essays about smoking and work on exercises that will assist you as you write your own. To help you, this preface will identify the main components of five-paragraph essays (as well as longer pieces) and discuss how these components fit together. It will also examine various kinds of descriptive writing and techniques that writers use to depict processes, places, and events.

Components of the Five-Paragraph Essay

An essay is a short piece of writing that discusses or analyzes one topic. Essays are commonly organized with a "tell, show, and summarize" pattern. First, the writer makes a "telling" statement expressing a point of view. Then, after "showing" by using examples and supporting arguments, the writer concludes by briefly summarizing what has been told and shown.

Five-paragraph essays are a form typically used in school assignments and tests. Every five-paragraph essay begins with an introduction, ends with a conclusion, and features three supporting paragraphs in the middle.

The *introduction* usually presents the essay's topic and thesis statement. The *topic* is the issue or subject discussed in the essay. All of the essays in this book are about the same topic—smoking. The *thesis*, or thesis statement, is the argument or point the writer is trying to make about the topic. The essays in this text all have different thesis statements because they are making different arguments about smoking.

For most classroom essays, the thesis statement should clearly assert a particular point of view about the topic. The titles of the viewpoints in this book are good examples; they each present a specific argument or assertion about smoking. A focused thesis statement helps determine what will be in the essay; the subsequent paragraphs are spent developing and supporting its argument.

In addition to presenting the thesis statement, a well-written introductory paragraph captures the attention of the reader and explains why the topic is important. It may provide the reader with background information on the subject matter. It may also "preview" what points are covered in the following paragraphs.

The introduction is followed by three (or more) *supporting paragraphs*. These are the main body of the essay. Each paragraph presents and develops a discrete argument (subtopic) that supports the thesis statement of the entire essay. Each subtopic is then supported with its own facts, details, and examples. Writers use various kinds of material and details to support the topics of each paragraph. These may include statistics, anecdotes, descriptive details, quotations from people with special knowledge or expertise, and historical facts. A rule of writing is that specific and concrete examples are more convincing than vague, general, or unsupported assertions.

The *conclusion* is the paragraph that closes the essay. Also called the ending or summary paragraph, its function is to summarize or restate the main idea of the essay. It may recall an idea from the introduction or briefly examine the larger implications of the thesis.

Although the order of these component paragraphs is important, one does not have to write the five-paragraph essay in the order it appears. Some writing instructors urge students to decide on a thesis and write the introductory paragraph first. The advantage is that they can then use that paragraph to help structure the rest of the essay. Others suggest that students decide on a working thesis, decide on the three points used to support it, and write the supporting paragraphs first, before finishing with the introductory and summary paragraphs. That method could be more flexible; if a student researcher discovers that the facts and evidence he or she is finding go beyond, or even against, the working thesis, then the thesis statement could be reworded.

Essays with an Implied Thesis

In some cases, especially in descriptive and narrative essays written in the first person (from the "I" point of view), no one sentence can be singled out as the thesis statement. Instead, the essay has an implied thesis—a point of view made evident through the writer's strong use of descriptive details and examples. In Viewpoint 5, for instance, Dale Pray maintains that family and peers influenced his decision to smoke. However, he makes no explicit statement to this effect. Instead, he carefully recounts some specific childhood memories that enable the reader to clearly grasp the argument he is making.

Descriptive-Writing Techniques

An important element of descriptive writing is the use of images and specific and concrete details. *Specific* and *concrete* are the opposites of *general* and *abstract*. Descriptive writers want to give their readers a fuller understanding of the topic by focusing in on tangible details and by appealing to the five senses. Compare the following three columns of words to see examples of general nouns and their more specific variations.

General	More Specific	Most Specific
vegetation	flowers	yellow tulips
animal	dog	rottweiler
grocery item	snack food	pretzel sticks
sound	booming noise	thunder

The use of metaphors and similes can also enliven descriptive writing. A metaphor is a comparison between two objects that are dissimilar. In Viewpoint 2, Mario Vargas Llosa describes his college smoking with metaphors: "Drawing in the smoke and blowing it out, in rings or as a cloud that dissolved into dancing figures, was a great felicity: a companion, a support, a distraction, a stimulus." The act of smoking and a companion, among other things, are two dissimilar things that are compared. A simile is a metaphor that includes the prepositions *like* or *as*. In Viewpoint 6, for example, Christina Fletcher notes that "cigarettes were like makeup or a security blanket for me—they completed me."

Some descriptive essays make use of both scene and exposition. The scene is an element commonly seen in fiction and in creative writing. With scene, a writer describes an event with moment-by-moment detail, often including dialogue if people are involved. With exposition, a writer explains, summarizes, or concisely recounts events that occur between scenes. Scene is comparable to "showing," whereas exposition is similar to "telling." The paragraphs of descriptive essays, narrative essays, and short stories often alternate between passages of scene and exposition. In Viewpoint 6, for example, Fletcher opens her essay with a scene about finding a pack of cigarettes with her friend while walking home from school. The second paragraph, a passage of exposition, includes some background information about the author. This prepares the reader for the scene in the third paragraph in which the author recalls smoking her first cigarette.

The following section includes three different kinds of descriptive essays. Model Essay 1 incorporates examples and spatial-order description, in which the writer paints a setting for the reader and shows where things are located from an observer's perspective. Model Essay 2 uses details, metaphors, and similes to describe the long-term effects of cigarette smoking. Model Essay 3 is a descriptive personal essay that makes use of scene, dialogue, and exposition.

Some Pitfalls to Avoid

A descriptive essay should give the reader a clear impression of its subject. In doing so, a writer must carefully select the most relevant details. A few well-chosen details are more effective than dozens of extraneous ones. You want the reader to visualize what you are describing but not feel overloaded with information. The room you are sitting in now, for example, is likely full of numerous concrete and specific items. To describe the room in writing, however, you would want to choose perhaps only five vivid details that would help convey your impression of and attitude about it.

A writer should also be aware of the kinds of words he or she uses in descriptive passages. Modifying words like adjectives and adverbs can enhance descriptive writing, but they should be used sparingly. Generally, verbs and nouns are more powerful than adjectives and adverbs. The overuse of modifying words makes the writing seem "wordy" and unnatural. Compare the phrases in the following table to see the difference between wordy and concise language.

Wordy	Concise
bright green potted plant with thin leaves	fern
rolling around rapidly in brilliant, untamed magnificence	dancing in the wild splendor
she stopped extremely abruptly	she stopped

As you write your descriptive essay, keep in mind that a few well-chosen words and details are more effective than long, complex, adjective-ridden passages.

Tobacco Advertising Encourages Youths to Smoke

Editor's Notes This first model essay argues that tobacco companies are still targeting minors in their advertising. It is structured as a five-paragraph essay that uses descriptive details and examples to develop the argument. The thesis statement is the final sentence at the end of the first paragraph.

The next three paragraphs offer evidence to support the thesis. Paragraphs two and three are examples of spatial-order description, in which the writer uses relevant details to describe a setting or a place. In paragraph four, the writer cites specific examples that support the topic sentence.

Notice how the body paragraphs are organized. They each start with a general assertion before focusing on one supportive example. This example is then elaborated on with descriptive details or with additional illustrative examples. The paragraphs end with sentences that explain the significance of the examples and that clarify the paragraph's relevance to the essay's thesis. Thus, these paragraphs all follow a "tell, show, and summarize" pattern.

The sidebars provide further observations and questions to help you see how this essay is organized.

Every day more than four thousand Americans between the ages of twelve and seventeen start smoking, reports the Centers for Disease Control and Prevention. Teenagers cite many reasons—peer pressure, rebellion, even the desire to lose weight—for trying cigarettes. What they may not know, however, is that the tobacco industry spends at least $8 billion a year on advertising. As of 1998, tobacco companies may no longer use billboards,

The first two sentences tell the reader that the essay will discuss smoking.

The use of *however* in the third sentence signals that a contrasting point will be made.

69

cartoon characters, or logo-emblazoned clothing to advertise their products. Yet these companies continue to find clever and tricky ways to market their products to minors.

Cigarette ads can still be found in magazines that young people read, especially those devoted to music, entertainment, and women's fashion. A recent issue of *Glamour,* for example, includes an advertisement for Camel Turkish Gold. Spread across three full pages, the reader is drawn into a scene inside an exotic nightclub. Adorned with fringed lanterns, ferns, golden columns, and dark velvet drapes, the club's marble-floored interior suggests a luxurious desert oasis. In every corner, elegantly dressed couples laugh, clink champagne glasses, and smoke. The focus of the scene is a waitress—or is she a supermodel?—wearing a strapless golden dress and selling Camels from a cart. She leans close to a dark-haired Romeo, all smiles, all coyness, sharing a naughty secret as she lights his cigarette. Printed in white on the bottom of the page is the phrase "Pleasure to Burn." The advertisement suggests, "Smoke Camels and you will be one of these beautiful, sophisticated people." It is a message that would appeal to young girls wanting to feel stylish, attractive, and grown-up.

Magazines are not the only places where young people might encounter cigarette advertising. Convenience stores such as 7-Eleven, Circle-K, Quik Trip, and gas station minimarts continue to advertise cigarettes, although the ads are more subtle than in the days before the 1998 ban on youth-oriented marketing. One corner store in a southern California neighborhood offers a good example of this discreet advertising. Boxes of Camels, Marlboros, and Mistys, with large-print signs stating their price, are laid out in long rows behind the cash register. Like the rows of candy and bubble gum in the store's main aisles, the cigarettes are placed rather low and are unusually close to the floor, within easy view of a child. Above the cash register, however, a bright yellow sign announces, "Under 18 No Tobacco. Please Have Your ID Ready. We Card." While such announcements are meant to be a part of a youth antismoking strategy, Americans for

Nonsmokers' Rights argues that these signs and conflicting messages also emphasize the "taboo" quality of cigarettes: "Signs directed at young customers give the message that smoking is an adult initiation. The tobacco industry has identified 'the forbidden fruit' appeal as an important factor in adolescent experimentation." Young people wanting to feel grown-up and independent who come across the "We Card" sign placed above rows of cigarettes are receiving a secret invitation to break the rules by smoking.

How does this quote from an authority help to explain the significance of this paragraph's specific details?

Another way to make cigarettes attractive to children and teenagers is through the movie industry. According to researcher Stanton Glantz, 50 percent of G- and PG-rated movies show smoking, and 80 percent of PG-13 movies have characters who use tobacco. Even cartoon characters can be smokers. Cruella DeVille, the conniving and dislikable—but also very memorable—villain in the classic cartoon *101 Dalmatians,* is a chain-smoker. For an older crowd, science-fiction action movies like *Independence Day* show Will Smith playing a hip, alien-killing hero who loves cigars. And in the 1997 blockbuster *Titanic,* yet another film that remains popular among youths, the romantic lead characters played by Leonardo DiCaprio and Kate Winslet are smokers. Winslet's character smokes to rebel against the limited role of women in the early 1900s. During a raucous dance scene, for example, she takes a drag off of a man's cigarette, gleefully flaunting a "forbidden" activity. Tobacco critics argue that such scenes in hit movies make cigarettes appealing to youths. "As good as the anti-tobacco campaigns are, they cannot compete with one actor on the screen," says Susan Moses, director of the Harvard Tobacco Project.

What is the topic sentence for this paragraph?

The writer uses specific examples from popular films to make a point.

What authority is cited to support this paragraph's topic argument?

Most teenagers do not believe that they are affected by advertising. According to writer John DiConsiglio, however, "Advertising is complicated. It's not just a matter of see-the-ad-smoke-the-cigarette. Advertisers work hard to create an image around a product." By finding slick ways to suggest that cigarettes are pleasurable, glamorous, and taboo for children, tobacco companies still entice minors to give smoking a try.

How does the writer avoid simply repeating the thesis statement?

Exercise One

Create an Outline from an Existing Essay

It helps to create an outline of the five-paragraph essay before you write it. The outline can help you organize the information, arguments, details, and evidence you have gathered through research or observation.

For this exercise, create an outline that could have been used to write Model Essay 1. Breaking this completed essay down into outline form will familiarize you with how outlines can help to classify and arrange information.

Part of the outline has already been started to give you an idea of the assignment.

Outline

Write the essay's thesis.

I. First supporting argument: Eye-catching cigarette ads can still be found in magazines young people read.
   A. A recent issue of *Glamour* includes an advertisement for Camel Turkish Gold.
      1. An exotic nightclub with lanterns, ferns, columns, drapes, and marble floors suggests a desert oasis.
      2. In every corner, couples laugh, drink, and smoke.
      3. A beautiful waitress lights a man's cigarette.
      4. "Pleasure to Burn" is printed on the bottom of the page.
   B. This ad would appeal to girls wanting to feel stylish, attractive, and grown-up.
II. Second supporting argument: Convenience stores and mini-marts continue to advertise cigarettes.
   A.
      1.
      2. etc.
   B.
III. Third supporting argument
   A.
   B. etc.

Welcome to the World of Smoking

Editor's Notes This second model essay presents an argument against smoking. It is structured as a five-paragraph essay that describes a process. It examines how smoking often begins as a pleasurable habit that leads to poor health and serious illness. Three main stages of this process—enjoying the pleasures of smoking, having a dirty and unhealthy habit, and living with disease—are described in the essay's three supporting paragraphs. Each of these paragraphs includes information and supporting details taken from the research sources and Web sites offered in the appendices and the organizations list at the end of the book. The writer also makes ample use of personal observations, specific and concrete details, and metaphors and similes. The essay concludes with a paragraph that reinforces the central argument through the use of a relevant quote.

As you read this essay, take note of its components and how they are organized (the sidebars provide further explanation). Notice that this essay's thesis is in the final paragraph rather than in the introductory one. The writer also approaches the topic in a creative way by using a sarcastic tone and an imperative, second-person ("you"), voice. In addition, consider the following questions: How does the introduction engage the reader's attention? Does the writer's tone enhance or detract from the essay's thesis? Which descriptive details do you find to be the most effective?

So, you have decided to be a smoker! Welcome to the 25 percent of Americans who engage in this most glamorous of habits. Did you know that at least 80 percent of them were introduced to the slim nicotine delivery sticks before the age of eighteen? Of course you do. You no doubt recall your first draw—the smoke searing the back of your throat, the dizziness and light-headedness that

This kind of statistical information is available in Appendix A of this book.

gripped you, the nausea you swallowed down. Perhaps you went into a coughing fit, your eyes squinting and watering from the smoke, but you smiled anyway because *you could take it*. You were ready to seize all this revulsion and risk and abandon, hold it between your lips, and inhale. And the more you returned to the empty lot or alley or friend's backyard to smoke, the more likely it was that your relationship with cigarettes would grow into a long-term commitment.

Notice the use of metaphor in this paragraph's topic sentence, in which the habit of smoking is compared to a marriage.

This marriage to smoking promises you years of pleasure and satisfaction. Every time you take a drag from a cigarette, your bloodstream quickly absorbs nicotine through your lungs and distributes it throughout your body. The pearly breeze blows through you—an ethereal sprite bestowing secret gifts—and you are *lifted up*. Your mental powers, previously sluggish, find liberation and release. The world comes into focus and you feel wily, invincible, sharp as a spy. Last but not least, you look so drop-dead elegant! That cigarette adorns your hand like a bouquet of baby's breath. The smoke flows from your nostrils in silky silence, offering the perfect answer to all questions.

Where are the other metaphors and similes in this paragraph?

Over time, undoubtedly, you'll begin to notice some flaws in this long-term commitment. Inevitably you'll drop ashes on your clothes, your furniture, your floor, decorating your surroundings with permanent burn marks. Visitors to your home, seeing these marks out of the corners of their eyes, occasionally mistake them for cockroaches. Perhaps you'll also have a girlfriend or a boyfriend who mentions that kissing you is like licking the inside of an old ashtray. But such is the price of having a sophisticated habit. Beyond these social gaffes are some physical changes. Your skin will start to droop and sag and take on sallow gray overtones, and facial wrinkles will arrive years before their time. You will catch colds and flus very quickly, and it will take you longer to get over them. In fact, more often than not, you'll feel like you have some kind of respiratory ailment. Your first wak-

What is the topic sentence of this paragraph?

The writer uses a transitional sentence here before describing the physical effects of smoking.

ing moments will entail coughing up yellowish-brown sputum, which becomes increasingly difficult to do because the habit of smoking hinders your lungs' cleansing ability. Aerobic exercise will not agree with you because your diminished lung capacity makes you easily tired. A doctor may tell you to quit or at least cut down on smoking. But you will likely find this to be quite a challenge, as a cigarette has become the one sure thing that can relax you, clear your head, and restore your wit.

After decades have passed, your loyalty to cigarettes will present even greater challenges. Exposure to carcinogens in cigarette smoke could give you a variety of cancers. A high percentage of people who develop cancer of the larynx (the voice box), for example, are cigarette smokers. If you crave the opportunity to discover new things, the removal of a cancerous larynx offers you the chance to relearn how to talk by burping air through a hole in the front of your neck. With the assistance of a mechanical voice box, your new voice will be an electronic monotone. If you prefer more physical challenges, smoking-induced emphysema will require you to exert enormous amounts of energy coughing up thick chunks of mucus and phlegm. Because your lungs will be less elastic, your efforts to breathe will entail strenuous wheezing. Your fingertips will turn violet blue when you are unable to get enough oxygen into your bloodstream. You will also need to plan your every movement in advance, as you will find that just getting up out of a chair can cause shortness of breath. But your friends may consider you lucky that you somehow avoided an earlier death from cancer or heart disease, a fate that befalls many smokers.

Truth be told, your decision to avoid or abandon any commitment to smoking may be the most important health decision you ever make. Just ask writer David Cowles, who smoked for fifty years before being diagnosed with lung cancer and emphysema. In describing his recovery from his cancer operation in a *Newsweek* editorial, he points out, "I felt anything but lucky. For days after the operation I

> How does the first sentence in this paragraph serve as a transition from the previous paragraph?

> Using information gathered from research, the writer briefly describes some effects of smoking-induced diseases.

> This is the essay's thesis sentence. Why is it in the final paragraph?

was in such horrendous pain I believed I'd never leave the hospital alive. For more than a month the excruciating pain returned. Even now, I am still very short of breath. Yes, I genuinely enjoyed smoking. But I certainly wish that I had found my pleasure elsewhere."

Exercise Two
Organize and Write Your Own Five-Paragraph Descriptive Essay

The second model essay includes descriptive passages that support a particular point of view about the effects of smoking. For this exercise, your assignment is to find supporting ideas, choose specific and concrete details, create an outline, and ultimately write a five-paragraph essay about factors that influence people to smoke or to avoid smoking. Your goal is to use descriptive detail in a persuasive essay that clearly asserts an opinion.

Step 1: Write a Thesis Statement

Examine the following thesis statements and choose one as the focus of your essay.

- Family and friends often influence a young person's decision to smoke.
- Family and friends often influence a young person's decision to avoid smoking.
- Antitobacco organizations help to reduce youth smoking.
- Antitobacco organizations do not reduce youth smoking.
- Youth smoking is an expression of rebellion.
- Youth smoking is an expression of conformity.

Using information from some of the viewpoints in the previous section and from the appendices in this book, write down three arguments that support the thesis statement you selected. Then, for each of these three arguments, write down supportive facts, examples, and details, again drawing from the sources available in this book or in your local library. This information could include:

- statistical information,
- personal memories and anecdotes,
- direct quotes from the viewpoints,
- observations of people's actions and behaviors,
- specific and concrete details,
- and quotes from peers and family members.

Here is a sample supporting argument for the thesis statement "Antitobacco organizations help to reduce youth smoking," followed with a list of supportive assertions and a relevant quote.

Antitobacco ads attract the attention of young people:

- youths help to write some of them (from Peter Vilbig, viewpoint 4)
- they appeal to a teenager's desire not to be hoodwinked (Vilbig)
- they use dark humor and sarcasm (Vilbig)
- one ad features a man selling popsicles with broken glass in them, hinting that people who sell tobacco are trying to make a dangerous product appealing (observation of television ad)
- "The 'truth' brand builds a positive, tobacco-free identity through hard-hitting advertisements that feature youths confronting the tobacco industry. This rebellious rejection of tobacco and tobacco advertising channels youths' need to assert their independence and individuality." (quote from Matthew C. Farrelly et al., *American Journal of Public Health,* 2002)

Step 2: Organize the Information in Outline Form

Thesis statement: Antitobacco organizations help to reduce youth smoking.

    I. First supporting argument
        A. Example, detail, statistic, or quote
        B. Example, detail, statistic, or quote
    II. Second supporting argument
        A. Example, detail, statistic, or quote
        B. Example, detail, statistic, or quote
    III. Third Supporting argument
        A. Example, detail, statistic, or quote
        B. Example, detail, statistic, or quote

Step 3: Write the Arguments in Paragraph Form

You now have three arguments that support the paragraph's thesis statement as well as supporting material. Use the outline to help you write out your three supporting arguments in paragraph form. Each paragraph has a topic sentence that states the paragraph's thesis and supporting sentences that express the facts, details, and examples that back up the paragraph's argument. The paragraph may also have a concluding or summary sentence.

Be aware of how you organize your examples and descriptive details within each paragraph. In Model Essay 1, the writer follows a general-to-specific pattern for each of the body paragraphs, beginning with a topic sentence and following up with supportive examples and details. The descriptive details themselves are also carefully ordered. Since people, places, and objects exist in space, the writer needs to decide whether to describe something from top to bottom, left to right, far to near, and so on. For example, the details in the second paragraph of Model Essay 1 are arranged in a far-to-near pattern. The writer first gives a kind of panoramic view of a nightclub featured in a tobacco advertisement: its lavish decor and the elegantly dressed couples standing in the background. Then the writer zeroes in on the one couple that is the focal point of the advertisement.

In the third paragraph of Model Essay 1, the writer opts for a bottom-to-top description of tobacco displays in a convenience store. Notice that the writer does not disrupt the ordering of details to return to an item that was passed up:

Not this: Boxes of Camels, Marlboros, and Mistys, with large-print signs stating their price, are laid out in long rows behind the cash register. Above the cash register, however, a bright yellow sign announces, "Under 18 No Tobacco. Please Have Your ID Ready. We Card." Like the rows of candy and bubble gum in the main aisles, the cigarettes are placed low, close to the floor, within easy view of a child.

But this: Boxes of Camels, Marlboros, and Mistys, with large-print signs stating their price, are laid out in long rows behind the cash register. Like the rows of candy and bubble gum in the store's main aisles, the cigarettes are placed low, close to the floor, within easy view of a child. Above the cash register, however, a bright yellow sign announces, "Under 18 No Tobacco. Please Have Your ID Ready. We Card."

Step 4: Write an Introduction and a Conclusion

The introducing and concluding paragraphs can greatly improve your essay by quickly imparting to your reader the essay's main idea. Well-written introductions grab the attention of the reader and reveal why the topic being explored is important and interesting. The conclusion often reiterates the thesis statement, but it is also the last chance for the writer to make an impression on the reader and to drive home his or her argument.

While the thesis statement commonly appears in the first paragraph of a five-paragraph essay, descriptive essay writers may, for creative effect, place it in the concluding paragraph. In Model Essay 2, for example, the writer focuses on specific details in the first four paragraphs of an essay describing a process. By placing the thesis in the last paragraph, a writer can create a suspenseful, "page-turner" effect because the reader must read to the end to see the writer's complete argument. Thus, instead of the common "tell, show, and summarize" pattern, a descriptive writer might use a "show, tell, and summarize" structure.

The Introduction

There are several techniques you can use in the opening paragraph to attract the reader's attention, including the following ones:

- An anecdote: A brief story that illustrates a point relevant to the topic.
- A descriptive passage that is relevant to the topic, with details of sight, sound, touch, taste, and smell to engage the reader.
- Startling information: true and pertinent facts or statistics that illustrate the point of the essay. A brief opening assertion can then be elaborated upon over the next few sentences.
- Setting up and knocking down a position: Begin the essay with an assertion proponents of one side of a controversy believe, only to then raise questions about that assertion.
- General-to-specific structure: The first sentence or two introduce the topic in general terms, with each sentence becoming gradually more specific until you conclude with a thesis statement.

The Conclusion

The conclusion brings the essay to a close by summarizing or restating its main argument(s). Good conclusions go beyond simply repeating the argument, however. They also answer the reader's question of "so what?"—in other words, they tell why the argument is important to consider. Some conclusions may also explore the broader implications of the thesis argument. They may close with a quotation or refer back to an anecdote or event in the essay. In essays covering controversial topics, the conclusion should reiterate which side the essay is taking.

Ashes in the Food

Editor's Notes The following essay is a descriptive personal essay. It differs from the previous two in several ways. For one thing, it is longer than five paragraphs. In many instances, five paragraphs are not enough to fully develop an idea. Secondly, its thesis is implied rather than explicitly stated. And while the previous model essays were written from an objective or an imperative point of view, this one is written from the subjective, or first-person ("I"), point of view.

In this essay the writer explores how her mother's smoking habit influenced her own ambivalent relationship with cigarettes. Many of the techniques seen in narrative essays and short stories—exposition, scene, descriptive detail, and dialogue—are used. Indeed, the essay has a narrative, storytelling quality to it. Purely narrative essays, however, typically focus on dramatizing a significant onetime event. In a descriptive personal essay, a writer has more "room" to write about a series of related events or events recurring over time. Viewpoints 1, 5, and 6 from Section 1 are all examples of descriptive first-person essays that contain some narrative elements.

As you read this essay, take note of the writer's use of sensory details, metaphors, and dialogue. The sidebars provide additional information and pertinent questions.

As a child I relished waking up to the hot, salty smell of butter on the grill as my mother made pancakes. I thought of it as the odor of sunlight. It was a lovely way to emerge from sleep, knowing that a tasty breakfast was on the way. Sometimes, though, I would get up out of bed and head into the kitchen, only to have that buttery aroma undercut by the acrid smell of cigarette smoke. Usually Mom could hang on until after breakfast to have her first cigarette of the day, but on occasion she would have to

The writer opens with a scene depicting a recurring childhood event.

Where are the metaphors in this paragraph?

have one while she was preparing breakfast. A deft juggler, she could hold a cigarette in one side of her mouth, flip the pancakes, pour the orange juice, and talk all at the same time. But sometimes the ashes gathering at the end of her cigarette would get dangerously long. Then I would whine with irritation, "Mom! You're going to get ashes in the food!"

"That's right!" She would shoot back, one hand on her aproned hip. "That's the kind of thing that happens when you let cigarettes into your life! Ashes in your food! So don't you ever start smoking, unless you like that gritty taste of tar!"

Of course, I did not feel like I needed to be reminded of the evils of smoking. As a young girl I always hated that throat-clenching smell of cigarette smoke. Even worse than the ashes hovering over the pancakes were the rides to school during winter storms. Mom usually drove me in her Dodge, and we would have the windows rolled all the way up to keep the snow and freezing rain out of the car. But if the streets were slippery, Mom would get wrinkle-faced and tight-jawed with worry. Sooner or later, she would reach for a cigarette. That foul-smelling smoke would fill up the inside of the car. I would end up hovering on the far edge of my seat, holding my breath, and rolling down the window an inch in an attempt to get some fresh air. My face would get wet and I would eat some snowflakes; then I'd have to roll up the window to keep from getting cold. "Sweetheart, I'm really sorry," Mom would say as she quickly puffed away. "But it just goes to show you that you better never start smoking." She would flash me a quick grin. "It is a bad habit and your kids will hate riding in a car with you."

Often I'd ask her, "Why don't you quit?" After all, shouldn't she be following her own advice? Shouldn't she be trying to set a good example for her children? And shouldn't she be worried about us breathing the smoke that she exhaled?

"I know, honey. You're right," she would answer with a small smile. "I ought to quit, but it's just impossible for me. Fact is, I never should have started. Which is why I hope you never start."

Although I never smoked as a child, my mother's habit intrigued me. As bad as cigarette smoke smelled to me, I began to believe that it must have felt exquisite to inhale it straight from the filtered end of the cigarette, or else people wouldn't get so addicted to it. My mother had a stressful job as a nurse, and smoking seemed to calm her down and keep her cheerful. Sometimes I was tempted to sneak a cigarette out of the pack of Kents she would leave sitting on the coffee table in our living room, light it, take a puff, and throw it in the trash outside. But I was always afraid that the smell of my breath would give me away. Instead, I would take a deep whiff of a freshly opened package of Kents from time to time. My mother preferred menthol, and her unsmoked cigarettes smelled like a mixture of mint and cedar. It was a pleasant fragrance, and I wondered if smoking was a way of taking that sweet, rich odor deep into the lungs.

As I discovered as an adult living half a continent away from home, smoking was not anything like inhaling perfumed incense. However, I did find, much to my mother's regret, that smoking felt good—at least initially. When I first began smoking, I enjoyed the light-headed "buzz" it would give me, followed by a sense of relaxed alertness. But as I became a more habitual smoker (smoking a little more than half a pack a day), these good feelings disappeared. I noticed that without my regularly scheduled cigarette, traffic, deadlines, television news, and simple conversation made me cranky and jittery. Even worse, I developed a constant cough and got easily winded. Although I did not have what is generally considered a "heavy" habit, I felt like I had a cold or bronchitis much of the time. So after two years, I quit smoking.

And yet I didn't *really* quit. On occasion, perhaps at a friend's party or in the company of coworkers who smoked, I would still smoke a cigarette now and then. I became what is known as a social smoker, a person who

How does the writer reveal her mixed feelings about smoking?

The following two paragraphs of exposition do more "telling" than "showing" as they reveal the writer's relationship with smoking.

smokes from time to time rather than daily. I prided myself on being able to enjoy the pleasures of smoking without being addicted to nicotine.

Sometimes I would even smoke with my mother on holiday visits back home. In her later years, Mom's favorite evening pastime was to sit at the kitchen table with a crossword puzzle, drinking tea and smoking. I would join her for this nightly ritual, working on some of the more difficult clues and bumming an occasional cigarette from her. She would scowl at me in her good-natured way as she handed me her lighter, saying, "Didn't I always warn you about this horrible habit?"

I'd take a puff and shake my head. "Oh Mom, don't worry, I hardly ever smoke."

"Hmmpf," she'd grunt. "That's what I said when I was young. And here I am now, breathing a pack a day."

I'd move the lit end of my cigarette close to her cup of tea, pretending like I was going to use it for an ashtray, and say, "If you keep it up I'll put ashes in your food!"

After age sixty or so, my mother had worked hard to cut down on her smoking. I noticed that she began smoking Ultra Golden Light Kents, a very low-tar choice, and that she also smoked less than half of each cigarette. She may have still gone through a pack each day, but overall she was smoking less than she used to. Her efforts seemed to pay off. Her only serious health problem was high blood pressure, which she controlled with medication and daily exercise. According to her doctor, her lungs were "clear" and "holding up." Although the U.S. surgeon general was constantly warning the public about the harms of cigarette smoking, I began to wonder if the dire reports about smoking and lung damage were overstated.

Then I got that late-night phone call from my sister Sara, who still lived near Mom. Our mother had had a mild heart attack and was in the hospital. Apparently she had called Sara, first complaining of nausea and tightness in her chest, but then insisting that she felt better after sitting down to smoke a cigarette! "Mom, I think I better come and take you to a doctor," Sara had said to her.

How does the exposition here lead into the scene?

Recalling an image from the essay's first scene provides a connecting thread and helps to show how the mother-daughter relationship has changed.

Why is the writer skeptical of health warnings about smoking?

"Oh, I'm okay now," was Mom's response. "At least I'm not feeling any pain in my arms." Pain in the left arm is a possible symptom of a heart attack—but so are nausea and chest tightness. Even though she had worked as a nurse, Mom didn't want to admit that she might have a life-threatening medical problem. My sister was rightly concerned and drove Mom to the closest emergency room. I flew home immediately.

My mother's heart attack was caused by several arterial blockages in her heart, and she needed to have a bypass operation to clear the arteries. When my sister and brother and I stood at her bedside before her surgery, she asked us to congratulate her because she had finally stopped smoking for an entire two days. The nurse had given her a nicotine skin patch to help control the cravings, and she was feeling better than she had in a long time—no longer so arthritic and dog-tired. The heart surgeon informed us that her prognosis was good. "Well," she said as I kissed her cheek before she was wheeled into surgery, "I guess that's finally it for ashes in the food!"

This brief snippet of dialogue again makes use of a significant recurring image.

Mom did not survive the operation. As the surgeon later told us, her heart tissue was much weaker than he had anticipated, and he was unable to get her heart pumping again after clearing out the clogged arteries. The damage to my mother's heart, he said, was likely the result of her many years of smoking.

We buried Mom with a book of crossword puzzles, a pencil, and her last pack of Kents. Cigarettes couldn't hurt her anymore now. Though her unexpected death was heartbreaking, we find comfort in the memory of her love, her spunky spirit, and her self-deprecating sense of humor. Have I decided to heed her wise smoker's warnings and abandon my every-now-and-then cigarette habit? Well, not quite. I still smoke perhaps three or four cigarettes a year. If you can hear me now, Mom, know this: I may flip those pancakes, but I keep no Kents in my house. Believe me, there will be no more chances of ashes in the food.

The author concludes by using the recurring image from the essay's first scene.

Practice Writing a Scene with Dialogue

Model Essay 3 uses scene, exposition, and dialogue to make a point. For this exercise, you will practice creative-writing techniques to draft a one- or two-paragraph scene with exposition.

With scene, a writer illustrates or dramatizes a moment in time. It is a form of "showing" rather than "telling." Specific and concrete details, metaphors and similes, action, and dialogue (if people are involved) all help to create scene and to make the writing vivid. In descriptive essays, writers may include scenes that depict recurring moments in time. Such is the case in the first paragraph of Model Essay 3, in which indicator words such as *sometimes* and *usually* show the recurrence of the writer waking up to the smells of breakfast and cigarette smoke.

The following paragraphs by freelance writer Susan Dominus offer an example of how a scene can serve as support for the argument that peer pressure encourages smoking. It is written from the objective, third-person, point of view:

So why do kids light up in the first place?

"Some friends of mine in seventh grade just said, 'Why don't we try it?'" says Paul, now a sophomore. His arm draped around Candace, he's wearing Cargo pants and is halfway through a cigarette. He's going to be handsome one day, but right now he's skinny, with a rash of acne across his chin only partly disguised by some sparse stubble. He holds a pack of Camels prominently in his hand, like a talisman, turning it upside down, tapping it on the sidewalk like a toy. "I thought, Well, if it's so bad for you, and people do it anyway, there must be something really great about it, right?"

Paul is in a band that's playing later at the town rec hall, and whenever a friend walks by, he calls after him, "See you tonight, right?" Every so often he coughs, making a harsh hacking sound. "I'm the sickliest kid," he admits. But he shrugs when asked if he's worried about getting seriously sick in the future, possibly as a result of smoking. "I'm not afraid of cancer," he says. "I believe in living fast and dying young."

"It's horrible," says Candace. "But there's something so sexy about cigarettes," Her face gets dreamy. "I like it when guys light a cigarette with a match and then flick it away. It's so destructive—so bad boy."

This scene is the result of the writer's interviews with and observations of certain individuals. Note the use of details, including articles of clothing, physical features, actions, gestures, and dialogue. The writer also uses similes ("holds a pack of Camels . . . like a talisman, . . . tapping it on the sidewalk like a toy"). Through these details and similes, the reader is drawn into a specific setting and moment in time.

With exposition, on the other hand, a writer explains, summarizes, or concisely recounts events that occur between scenes. Exposition, a form of "telling," may also help to transition into a scene—moving from general to specific—or to examine the significance of a scene. Take another look at Model Essay 3 and its sidebars to see how a writer alternates between passages of scene and exposition.

A Note on Dialogue
- Use natural-sounding language.
- Include a few details showing character gestures and expressions as they speak.
- Avoid overuse of speaker tags with modifiers, such as "he said stupidly," "she muttered softly," "I shouted angrily," and so on.
- Indent and create a new paragraph when speakers change.

- Place quotation marks at both the beginning and the end of a character's speech. Do not enclose each sentence of a speech in quotation marks.

Scene-Writing Practice
Interview a classmate, friend, or family member. Focus on a specific question about smoking, such as the following:

- Have you ever tried smoking? What was it like?
- Are you bothered by the smell of cigarette smoke? Why?
- Why do you think people start smoking?

Observe your interviewee and take notes as he or she answers. Write down what he or she says as well as details such as physical appearance, gestures, clothing, and so on. Use your notes to create a brief one- or two-paragraph scene with dialogue.

Exercise Four — Write a Descriptive Essay That Includes Scene and Exposition

The final exercise is to write your own descriptive essay on smoking that includes exposition and scene. It should be five paragraphs or longer. The resources in this book provide you with information about smoking and about descriptive-writing techniques.

Step 1: Deciding on the Topic
You may choose as the focus of your essay one of the following topics:

- the health effects of smoking
- public attitudes about smoking
- local bans on smoking in public places
- secondhand smoke

- girls/women and smoking
- nicotine addiction
- reducing/preventing tobacco use
- quitting smoking

Step 2: Write Down Questions, Answers, and Ideas
Here are some possible questions to help you think about your topic:

- Why is this topic important?
- Why should people be interested in this topic?
- What question am I going to answer in this paragraph or essay?
- How can I best answer this question?
- What facts, ideas, or examples can I use to support the answer to my question?
- Do I have any vivid memories connected with this topic?
- Do I know people who might have opinions or experience on this topic?
- How can I make this essay engaging for the reader?

Step 3: Gather Related Information
This volume contains several places to find information, including the viewpoints and the appendices. In addition, you may want to research the books, articles, and Web sites listed, or do additional research in your local library. Personal observations, experiences, and discussions with others might also supply you with information for your descriptive essay.

To help you develop scenes that you can use in your essay, you could:

- Interview peers or family members about your topic. Write down some direct quotes from them. Also jot down a few descriptive details pertaining to their appearance, facial expressions, mannerisms, and so on.

- Write notes about significant memories or experiences that you have had that are related to your topic.
- Observe people's behavior and jot down details of sight, sound, touch, taste, and smell.

Step 4: Develop Your Working Thesis

Use what you have written down in steps two and three to help you decide on the point you want to make in your essay.

For this essay you are not required to have an explicit thesis statement. In these planning stages, however, you should write out a "working thesis" to keep you on track as you compose your essay.

At this time you should also decide if you will be writing from the objective, imperative, or subjective point of view.

Step 5: Write a Rough Outline

1. Write down your working thesis at the top.

2. Write roman numerals I, II, III, and so on on the left side of the page.

3. Next to each roman numeral, write down the strongest ideas and arguments that you gathered in step three. These should all support your working thesis.

4. Under each roman numeral, use letters (A, B, C) to specify facts, information, quotes, observations, or personal experiences that support that particular argument.

5. As you arrange these arguments with their supporting examples and details, decide on what would be the best order for your ideas. Model Essay 3 uses chronological order: It begins with an early childhood memory and ends with a recent adulthood memory. Descriptive essays may also be written so that the supportive arguments are arranged from less significant to most significant. Arrange your ideas in a way that will keep your reader engaged from beginning to end.

Step 6: Write a Rough Draft

Write a rough draft of your essay, including at least one passage of both scene and exposition that support your working thesis. See Exercise 3 for information on writing scenes with exposition and dialogue.

Step 7: Read and Rewrite

- Does your first paragraph grab the reader's attention?
- Does the essay maintain a consistent tone?
- Do all sentences in some fashion reinforce your general thesis?
- Do paragraphs flow from one to the other? Do you need transition words or phrases?
- Do your scenes dramatize events that are relevant to your working thesis?
- Have you included details that appeal to sight, sound, touch, taste, and smell?
- Does the essay get bogged down in too much detail or irrelevant material?
- Are your details arranged in a clear order?
- Does the conclusion allow the reader to see why your point of view is important?
- Does your essay have a title?
- Are there any spelling or grammatical errors?

Section
Three:
Supporting
Research
Material

Facts About Smoking

Editor's Note: These facts can be used in reports or papers to reinforce or add credibility when making important points or claims.

General Facts

- Smoking causes at least four hundred thousand deaths annually in the United States. This is more than the number of people who die from AIDS, alcohol and drug abuse, traffic accidents, murders, suicides, and fires combined.
- On average, men who smoke cut their lives short by 13.2 years; women who smoke cut their lives short by 14.5 years.
- Cigarette smoke contains more than forty-seven hundred chemicals, more than two hundred poisons, and more than fifty human carcinogens.
- The list of diseases caused by smoking includes chronic lung diseases; periodontitis (gum disease); cardiovascular diseases; acute myeloid leukemia; cancers of the lung, stomach, throat, esophagus, larynx, bladder, kidney, pancreas, and cervix; and SIDS (sudden infant death syndrome).
- Smoking damages the airways and the alveoli of the lung, eventually leading to chronic bronchitis, emphysema, and chronic obstructive pulmonary disease—the fourth-leading cause of death in the United States.
- Smoking slows down lung growth, decreases lung function, and reduces the oxygen available for muscles.
- 90 percent of lung cancer cases are smoking related.
- 17 percent of adult lung cancers occur in people who never actively smoked but who grew up in a smoking household.
- Smoking raises cholesterol levels and white blood cell counts, which increases the risk of heart disease and heart attack.

- Secondhand smoke is responsible for fifty-three thousand deaths each year in the United States—thirty-seven thousand of them due to coronary artery disease.
- Tobacco companies spend about $8 billion a year on advertising.
- Antismoking groups spend about $800 million a year on antitobacco campaigns.
- Nearly 12.5 million acres of forest are destroyed each year to provide wooden containers for curing (drying) tobacco.

Annual Effects of Parental Smoking in the United States
- Low birth weight: forty-six thousand infants and twenty-eight hundred perinatal deaths
- Severe acute respiratory syndrome: two thousand deaths
- Lower respiratory infections: twenty-two thousand hospitalizations, eleven hundred deaths
- Ear infections: 3.4 million outpatient visits, 110,000 treatments with insertion of ear tubes
- Asthma: 1.8 million outpatient visits, fourteen deaths
- Fire-related injuries: ten thousand outpatient visits, 590 hospitalizations, 250 deaths.

Smoking and Youth
- Nearly 80 percent of adult smokers started smoking before age eighteen.
- More than half of adult smokers began smoking before age fourteen.
- Each day nearly three thousand youths under age eighteen become regular smokers.
- 4.5 million people under age eighteen are current smokers.
- One-third of youths who try smoking become regular smokers before leaving high school.
- 87 percent of teenage smokers prefer Marlboro, Newport, and Camel—the three most heavily advertised brands.

- 10.7 percent of eighth graders and 17.7 percent of tenth graders are current smokers.
- Researchers estimate that more than 5 million children alive today will die prematurely because of smoking.
- While nearly 80 percent of minors try cigarettes, about 25 percent become heavy smokers as adults.
- Nearly 60 percent of teens who have tried marijuana tried cigarettes first.
- 50 percent of G- and PG-rated movies show characters smoking, while nearly 80 percent of PG-13 rated movies contain tobacco use.
- 66 percent of movies that feature characters who smoke carry youth ratings of G, PG, or PG-13.
- 73 percent of top-selling movies show characters who use tobacco.

Finding and Using Sources of Information

When you write an essay for a class assignment, it is usually necessary to find information to support your point of view. You can use sources such as books, magazine articles, and online articles.

Using Books and Articles

You can find books and articles in a library by using the card catalog or the library's online catalog on a computer. If you are not sure how to use the card catalog or the library's computer, ask a librarian to instruct you. You can also use a computer to find many magazine articles and other articles written specifically for the Internet.

You are likely to find a lot more information than you can possibly use in your essay, so your first task is to narrow it down to what is likely to be most usable. Look at book and article titles. Look at book chapter titles, and examine the book index to see if the book contains information on the specific topic you want to write about. (For example, if you want to write about secondhand smoke and you find a book about the tobacco industry, check the chapter titles and index to be sure it contains information about secondhand smoke before you bother to check out the book.)

For a five-paragraph essay, you don't need a great deal of supporting information, so quickly try to narrow down your materials to a few good books and magazine or Internet articles. You don't need dozens. You might even find that one or two good books or articles contain all the information you need.

You probably don't have time to read an entire book, so find the chapters or sections that relate to your topic, and skim these. When you find useful information, copy it onto a notecard or notebook. You should look for supporting facts, statistics, quotations, and examples.

Evaluate the Source

When you select your supporting information, it is important that you evaluate its source. This is especially important with information you find on the Internet. Because nearly anyone can put information on the Internet, there is as much bad information as good information. Before using Internet information—or any information—try to determine if the source seems to be reliable. Is the author or Internet site sponsored by a legitimate organization? Is it from a government source? Does the author have any special knowledge or training relating to the topic you are looking up? Does the article give any indication of where its information comes from?

Using Your Supporting Information

When you use supporting information from a book, article, interview, or other source, there are three important things to remember:

1. Make it clear whether you are using a direct quotation or a paraphrase. If you copy information directly from your source, you are quoting it. You must put quotation marks around the information, and tell where the information comes from. If you put the information in your own words, you are paraphrasing it. Sometimes you must tell where you found this information too.

   Here is an example of using a quotation:

   According to the U.S. Centers for Disease Control, a government agency that works to protect national and global health, "Events and activities popular among young people are often sponsored by tobacco companies. Free tickets to films and to pop and rock concerts have been given in exchange for empty cigarette packets in Hong Kong and Taiwan. Popular U.S. female stars have allowed their names to be associated with cigarettes in other countries."[1]

1. Centers for Disease Control and Prevention, "Marketing Cigarettes to Women—Fact Sheet," March 2005, www.cdc.gov.

Here is an example of a brief paraphrase of the same passage:

According to the U.S. Centers for Disease Control, a government agency that works to protect national and global health, tobacco companies often promote movies, concerts, and pop stars as a way to market cigarettes to youths.

2. Use the information fairly. Be careful to use supporting information in the way the author intended it. There is a joke that movie ads containing critics' comments like "First-Class!" "Best ever!" and other glowing phrases taken from longer reviews that said something like "This movie is first-class trash" or "This movie is this director's best ever—and that isn't saying much!" This is called *taking information out of context* (using it in a way the original writer did not intend). This is using supporting evidence unfairly.

3. Give credit where credit is due. You must give credit when you use someone else's information, but not every piece of supporting information needs a credit.
   - If the supporting information is general knowledge—that is, it can be found in many sources—you do not have to cite (give credit to) your source.
   - If you directly quote a source, you must give credit.
   - If you paraphrase information from a specific source, you must give credit.

   If you do not give credit where you should, you are *plagiarizing*—or stealing—someone else's work. There are a number of ways to give credit. Your teacher will probably want you to do it one of three ways:
   - Informal: As in the examples in number 1 above, you tell where you found the information in the same place you use it.

- Informal list: At the end of the article, place an unnumbered list of the sources you used. This tells the reader where, in general, you obtained your information, but it doesn't tell specifically where you found any single fact.
- Formal: Use a footnote, like the first example in number 1 above. (A footnote is generally placed at the bottom of the page, although it may be located in different places depending on your teacher's requirements.)

Be sure you know exactly what information your teacher requires before you start looking for your supporting information so that you know what information to include with your notes.

Sample Essay Topics

Working Thesis Statements for Descriptive and Persuasive Essays

Smoking Has Serious Health Effects

The Dangers of Smoking Have Been Exaggerated

Secondhand Smoke Is Harmful to Health

The Harmful Effects of Secondhand Smoke Have Been Exaggerated

The Tobacco Industry Is Responsible for Smoking-Related Illnesses

The Tobacco Industry Is Not Responsible for Smoking-Related Illnesses

Tobacco Advertising Persuades People to Smoke

Tobacco Advertising Does Not Persuade People to Smoke

Peer Pressure Persuades Teens to Smoke

Smoking Is an Expression of Rebellion

Smoking Is an Expression of Conformity

Tobacco Use Among Teens Is a Serious Problem

Tobacco Use Among Teens Is Not a Serious Problem

Antismoking Campaigns Help Reduce Youth Smoking

Antismoking Campaigns Make Tobacco More Attractive to Youths

The Entertainment Industry Glamorizes Smoking

Smoking Should Be Regulated by the Government

Smoking Should Not Be Regulated by the Government

Quitting Smoking Is Difficult

Quitting Smoking Is Not Difficult

Organizations to Contact

Action on Smoking and Health (ASH)
2013 H St. NW, Washington, DC 20006
(202) 659-4310 • Web site: www.ash.org

Action on Smoking and Health promotes the rights of non-smokers and works to protect them from the harms of smoking. The organization publishes fact sheets on a variety of topics, including teen smoking, passive smoking, and nicotine addiction.

American Cancer Society
1599 Clifton Rd. NE, Atlanta, GA 30329
toll-free: (800) ACS-2345 (227-2345)
Web site: www.cancer.org

The society spends a great deal of its resources on educating the public about the dangers of smoking and on lobbying for antismoking legislation.

American Lung Association (ALA)
61 Broadway, 6th Floor, New York, NY 10006
(212) 315-8700 • toll-free: (800) 548-8252
e-mail: info@lungusa.org • Web site: www.lungusa.org

The American Lung Association is dedicated to the prevention, cure, and control of all types of lung disease, including asthma, emphysema, and lung cancer.

Americans for Nonsmokers' Rights
2530 San Pablo Ave., Suite J, Berkeley, CA 94702
(510) 841-3032 • fax: (510) 841-3071
e-mail: anr@no-smoke.org • Web site: www.no-smoke.org

Americans for Nonsmokers' Rights seeks to protect the rights of nonsmokers in the workplace and other public settings.

Campaign for Tobacco-Free Kids

1400 Eye St., Suite 1200, Washington, DC 20005
(202) 296-5469 • e-mail: info@tobaccofreekids.org
Web site: www.tobaccofreekids.org

The Campaign for Tobacco-Free Kids is the largest private initiative ever launched to protect children from tobacco addiction.

Canadian Council for Tobacco Control (CCTC)

75 Albert St., Suite 508, Ottawa, ON K1P 5E7 Canada
toll-free: (800) 267-5234 • (613) 567-3050
fax: (613) 567-2730 • e-mail: info-services@cctc.ca
Web site: www.cctc.ca

The CCTC works to ensure a healthier society, free from addiction and involuntary exposure to tobacco products. Its Web site features a Tobacco Control Reference Catalogue.

Children Opposed to Smoking Tobacco (COST)

Mary Volz School, 509 W. 3rd Ave., Runnemede, NJ 08078
e-mail: costkids@costkids.org • Web site: www.costkids.org

COST was founded in 1996 by a group of middle-school students committed to keeping tobacco products out of the hands of children.

Environmental Protection Agency (EPA)

Indoor Air Quality Information Clearinghouse
PO Box 37133, Washington, DC 20013-7133
toll-free: (800) 438-4318 • (703) 356-4020
fax: (703) 356-5386 • e-mail: iaqinfo@aol.com
Web site: www.epa.gov

The EPA is the agency of the U.S. government that coordinates actions designed to protect the environment. It promotes indoor air quality standards that reduce the dangers of secondhand smoke.

Fight Ordinances & Restrictions to Control & Eliminate Smoking (FORCES International)

Contact Person: Audrey Silk, PO Box 1036, Brooklyn, NY 11234 • (530) 690-8990 • e-mail: info@forces.org
Web site: www.forces.org

FORCES is a nonprofit, member-supported organization with chapters in the United States, Canada, Europe, and New Zealand. It opposes any state or local ordinance it feels is not fair to those who choose to smoke.

Group Against Smoking Pollution (GASP)

PO Box 632, College Park, MD 20741-0632
(301) 459-4791

GASP works to promote the rights of nonsmokers, to educate the public about the problems of secondhand smoke, and to encourage the regulation of smoking in public places.

The Tobacco Institute

Web site: www.tobaccoinstitute.com

As a result of the tobacco settlement of 1998, the institute's Web site currently gives the public free access to documents—many of them previously confidential—relevant to lawsuits against the tobacco industry.

Bibliography

Books

Karen F. Balkin, ed., *Tobacco and Smoking: Opposing Viewpoints.* San Diego: Greenhaven Press, 2005.

John Crofton and David Simpson, *Tobacco: A Global Threat.* New York: Macmillan Education, 2002.

William Douglass, *The Health Benefits of Tobacco: A Smoker's Paradox.* Miami, FL: Rhino, 2004.

Iain Gately, *Tobacco: A Cultural History of How an Exotic Plant Seduced Civilization.* New York: Grove Press, 2003.

Michael G. Goldstein et al., *The Tobacco Dependence Treatment Handbook: A Guide to Best Practices.* New York: Guilford Press, 2003.

John Harvey and M.D. Kellogg, *Tobaccoism; or How Tobacco Kills.* Kita, MT: Kessinger, 2003.

Leonard A. Jason et al., eds., *Preventing Youth Access to Tobacco.* Binghamton, NY: Haworth Press, 2003.

David Kessler, *A Question of Intent: A Great American Battle with a Deadly Industry.* New York: Public Affairs, 2002.

C.J. Westerfield, *The Cost of Using Tobacco.* Bloomington, IN: First Books Library, 2002.

Periodicals

Catherine Arnst, "The Skinny on Teen Smoking," *Business Week,* December 2, 2002.

Suzanne Batchelor, "Movie Smoking Hooks Teens, Experts Say," *National Catholic Reporter,* February 6, 2004.

Black Issues in Higher Education, "Hip-Hop Images Blamed for Seducing Minority Youth into Smoking," September 9, 2004.

Susan Dominus, "Teens and Tobacco: A Love Story," *Good Housekeeping,* November 2002.

James Gerstenzang, "Health Risks from Smoking More Widespread, Report Says," *Los Angeles Times,* May 28, 2004.

Diana Gordon, "Too Many Kids Smoke," *State Legislatures,* March 2004.

Cathy Gourley, "Smoke Screens on the Big Screen," *Current Health 2,* February 2004.

Sean McCollum, "Up in Smoke: Smoking Harms Your Health and Empties Your Wallet," *Scholastic Choices,* February/March 2004.

Maryann Napoli "Low Tar Cigarettes Not Safer," *HealthFacts,* January 2002.

Pamela Sherrid, "Smokers' Revenge," *U.S. News & World Report,* November 4, 2002.

Sidney Zion, "The Big Lie of Secondhand Smoke," *San Francisco Examiner,* November 29, 2002.

Index

Picture Credits

Cover Image: © Benjamin Rondel/CORBIS; AP/Wide
    World Photos (inset)
AFP/Getty Images, 54
AP/Wide World Photos, 29, 41
© Bettmann/CORBIS, 12, 49
© CORBIS, 47
© Dan Smith/Colombia/SKA Films/The Kobal
    Collection, 37
Getty Images, 15, 26, 32
© Joe Sharpnack, 25
© Jose Luis Pelaez/CORBIS, 56
© Kirk, 50
© Lee Snider/Photo Images/CORBIS, 34
© Mike Peters, 35
© Photo Researchers, Inc., 19, 57
Royalty Free/Getty Images, 22
© Scott Houston/CORBIS SYGMA, 43
Suzanne Santillan, 14, 59
Victor Habbick, 13, 20, 44
© Wolverton, 21

About the Editor

Mary E. Williams earned a master of fine arts degree from San Diego State University, where she studied comparative literature, poetry, and creative writing. Williams has an enduring interest in race relations, world religions, and social justice. An editor for Greenhaven Press since 1996, she lives in San Marcos, California, with her husband, Kirk Takvorian.